The
ONE MINUTE
CHRISTIAN

The
ONE MINUTE
CHRISTIAN

GROWING TOWARD
TRUE SPIRITUALITY

DON HAWKINS

MOODY PRESS
CHICAGO

ISBN: 0-8024-6196-4

1 3 5 7 9 10 8 6 4 2

Printed in the United States of America

FOREWORD

The nature of my business and life is such that I encounter people who occupy virtually every station in life. A high percentage of them are climbing the ladder of success. I share with these people, just as Don Hawkins is sharing, that success is measured by more than the checkbook; that money, for example, will buy a house but not a home. It will buy a bed but not a good night's sleep, a companion but not a friend, pleasure but not happiness, a piece of real estate but not peace of mind. Since everybody wants these things in addition to financial success, I relate very much to the compelling message in *The One Minute Christian*.

Ever since I committed my life to Jesus Christ on the July Fourth weekend of 1972, I've been spreading the word that true success and Christian faith aren't incompatible. I'm convinced that the stairway to the top—there is no elevator —consists of such steps as attitude, goals, self-image, relationships, desire, and work. As this book points out, all of these are at their best when authentic spirituality is present.

I'm also delighted with the way Don Hawkins shows that, although success comes through applying simple, basic principles, there are no shortcuts and you can't get a "square deal" by "cutting corners." *The One Minute Christian* gently but firmly knocks the props out from under our fast-food, microwave society's approach, which demands everything right now.

Finally, I appreciate how the older character mentors the young man. As a young salesman I had the advantage of having a mentor, Bill Crawford, who was my sales manager and friend. He exercised the proverbial patience of Job with me, believed in me, and taught me many strategic lessons on sales, leadership, and life. Don Hawkins's book brings the process of mentoring to life.

Don't let the fact that I'm an optimist by nature fool you into discounting my hearty recommendation of *The One Minute Christian*. This is a book that hits the bull's-eye about what matters more than anything else in life.

And if you apply its message in *your* life, then I'll really SEE YOU AT THE TOP—the real top.

ZIG ZIGLAR

ACKNOWLEDGMENTS

The One Minute Christian is the outgrowth of the encouragement and input of many individuals.

My special thanks to Kathy—my best friend, wife, and partner in our varied endeavors—and to Karen, Donna, and Brent for their unique ways of encouraging me.

An extra word of appreciation to Ruth Franks for typing and retyping the many words that make up this work.

A note of gratitude to Jim Bell, Duncan Jaenicke, Joe O'Day, Anne Scherich, Ella Lindvall, and the rest of the editorial and production staff of Moody Press for significant input into this project from start to finish, and to Dr. Joseph Stowell for believing in me and in the project.

A final word of gratitude to all whose lives, beliefs, and ideas contributed to the book and its characters. These include Kenneth Blanchard and Spencer Johnson, as well as Gary, Scott, Bill, and Greg for input and encouragement along the way.

THE SEARCH

Once there was a sharp young man who was on his way up. He was part of the generation called the baby boomers. Some people would have referred to him as a yuppie. Happily married to his college sweetheart, he wanted the very best out of life. To all appearances, this young man was extremely successful. Those who observed his life predicted even greater success in the future.

Several years before, he had completed his college education, graduating *summa cum laude*. Although physically not large enough for college football, he had played basketball. More important, he had also been elected president of the student body.

He then successfully pursued a master's degree in business administration from a noted graduate school of business. With his coveted MBA in hand he applied to a number of successful corporations and was immediately hired by a Fortune 500 company. Quickly establishing his reputation as a hard worker and a quick study, he began advancing through the corporate ranks, taking on new projects, working long hours, showing dedication to the company's objectives. His philosophy was "whatever it takes, I'll be successful in this company." Without question, he was on his way up. The young man's personal credo could be expressed under such tenets as, "Work hard, play hard, acquire for the future, enjoy the present."

Like many in his baby boomer generation, the young man was a consumer. Shortly after his first raise, he handed the keys to his Japanese sports sedan to his wife and leased one of the ultimate German driving machines—a BMW 735i. He waited two months to obtain the exact color he wanted—"Platinum. To match my platinum American Express card," he bragged. Actually the young man had a fistful of credit cards, some platinum, some gold (both VISA and MasterCard)—"after all, you never knew when you might need more credit."

On the recommendation of one of his co-workers, the young man began buying monogrammed, hand-tailored shirts. He developed a taste for Italian suits. ("Armani looks the best on me.") He was dressed for success. Both the young man and his wife enjoyed shopping—they were the consummate consumers.

Outwardly the young man and his wife seemed happy and successful, enjoying life to the hilt— the ultimate yuppie couple.

Shortly after his second promotion—with another substantial salary increase—he and his wife moved into a new custom home on a lake just outside the city. His wife began filling the home with designer furniture and antiques. The man purchased a state-of-the-art home entertainment system, including a large-screen television with stereo hi-fi VCR and a satellite dish for ultimate channel reception, and incredibly sophisticated audio equipment including a programmable carousel CD changer and a dual auto-reverse audio cassette deck.

The young couple purchased a ski boat with a powerful inboard engine, although they seldom found time to enjoy it. The man was extremely busy with his career, not to mention attending professional football, baseball, and basketball games, or watching them on his home entertainment system. Meanwhile the woman, while wrapped up in her career as an architect, was devoting many hours to volunteer work at the local museum.

Outwardly the young man and his wife seemed happy and successful, enjoying life to the hilt—the ultimate yuppie couple. They were living proof that "you can have it all." They lived by the motto "You deserve the best." They were working hard, living fast, playing hard.

This young man had grown up in a home that could best be described as middle class. His father worked in a steel mill—put in a lot of overtime. His mother did occasional secretarial work, but for the most part stayed home. The young man's dad was, like many men of his generation, stronger on work than on relationships. He constantly pushed the young man to work hard, to succeed, to be the best at school and at sports, and to get a job at an early age.

Following his dad's advice, the young man began working in a gasoline station when he was ten. He did well in school and brought home good grades—but from his dad's perspective, they were never good enough. In fact, the young man's dad seemed to subscribe to the motto "You spoil a kid by praising him—you motivate a kid by criticizing him."

The young man's parents both attended church regularly, although he perceived his mother to be more deeply religious than his dad. Similar to the local country club, church was a place where the right people gathered for the right kinds of activities. They were challenged to do good deeds, exhorted about social justice, motivated to help the poor and disadvantaged. Like many of his peers, the young man at an early age had been "confirmed," and his name added to the roll of the church. He attended youth activities, sang with other white-robed boys and girls, and listened to hundreds of lengthy sermons delivered in stentorian tones by robed ministers who seldom said anything that really grabbed his attention.

Beginning in his high school years and continuing into college, the young man became less concerned with matters of personal faith. He began to focus on simply living life to the hilt. He cultivated the "go for the gusto" mentality he constantly heard on the beer commercials that accompanied the sporting events he watched. When he went out for football, he found that most of the guys believed drinking beer to be the ultimate test of manhood. Throughout high school and college, the young man became known as a "party animal" who could down a six-pack without it downing him. From post-game parties to spring break "beach blasts" in Florida, he began to consume what he considered to be the pleasures of life—alcohol, sex, and an occasional marijuana cigarette, though he prided himself on never touching the hard drugs. His involvement in these activities caused his parents no end of grief and led to frequent unpleasant confrontations.

During his college years the young man, following the lead of many of his professors, adopted a hostile attitude toward Christianity. He considered himself more scientific than Christians, more sophisticated. Yet, though he asserted that humanism and the scientific method rather than Christianity provided the basis for dealing with truth, the real issue for the young man was his lifestyle. He figured if he ever became a Christian, he would have to give up something he liked. That just wasn't part of his plan.

However, during his last year in college, he became friends with two young men, members of his fraternity, who were actively involved in a Christian organization on campus. They invited the young man to attend their Bible studies and discussion groups. He became fascinated with their perspective on faith and the answers they had to some of the questions his professors had raised. He didn't agree with everything they said. In fact, he ridiculed their approach. Often he argued that they simply used Christ as a crutch. But he listened.

It was at this time that he began seeing the young lady he would eventually marry. They had dated a few times during his senior year in high school, and he had known her since childhood. She and her parents were members of the same church he attended—in fact, she had first caught his eye during church youth activities. She wasn't like the "easy girls" who had been so much a part of his earlier college life. She resisted his sexual advances—and he respected her for it. A girl of high moral character, she made clear that she was "saving herself for marriage." She seemed to take church a bit more seriously than he did, but she didn't preach at him, nag him, or scold him. He considered her to be more of a Christian than he was—although she never chided him when, in response to her question, he asserted, "Sure, I'm a Christian. I was baptized when I was a child."

It didn't take the young man long to sense that he wasn't really satisfied with where he was—either in the business world or in life.

The couple married in their childhood church shortly after they completed their college education. It was the social event of the year—attended by hundreds of family and friends.

During the early years of their marriage, both attended church fairly regularly. When asked, the young man referred to himself and his wife as Christians. But soon the pressures of graduate school caused the young man to attend church less and less often. A short time after he received his MBA and his first position, the young man and his wife found themselves with more money than they had ever imagined. They began taking weekend trips, or they stayed home on weekends to "unwind from the pressures of the week" and to enjoy all the nice new toys they were buying.

It didn't take the young man long to sense that he wasn't really satisfied with where he was—either in the business world or in life. Something was missing. He just wasn't sure what. He began reading some of the numerous books available on self-help, spirituality, and personal growth.

Many of these writings challenged him, some even excited him. None really helped him get where he wanted to be.

As he scanned the skies with his satellite dish, occasionally he ran across individuals who subscribed to his personal life motto: "You can have it all." One television preacher in particular fascinated him. This man's message could be summed up as "Support me, and God will bless you with great wealth." It was obvious from the cut of his clothes, his message, the flashy jewelry that adorned his attractive young wife, and his lavish television studio that he was extremely successful.

For a time the young man responded to this preacher's message. But finally he decided, "They're just after my money." So he wrote the preacher and asked that his name be dropped from the mailing list.

At this point the young man became even more cynical about spiritual things. At the core of his being he felt a need to please God—and he sensed that things in his relationship with God weren't right. But God seemed distant—sort of like his father had been—and although he really wanted to please God, he didn't want anything, not even God, to interfere drastically with his personal lifestyle.

One day, a friend from his college days—one of the fraternity mates who had been involved in a Bible study— invited him to attend a conference. He attended, but he spent the entire weekend verbally challenging everything he was hearing. At one point he exclaimed, "This guy's trying to tell me that God wants me to do some kind of ministry or go to a mission field to serve him. He doesn't understand. I can serve a lot better right where I am." What the young man didn't say to his friend was what he was really thinking: *There's no way I'm going to even consider letting God or anybody else mess with my good life.*

But the young man did decide to start attending church again on a regular basis. He figured that was what it would take to please God. He began dropping regular checks in the offering plate—after all, his cash flow was pretty good, and his CPA told him he could use a few more tax deductions. His wife was pleased with his new interest in church.

As for his own motivation, he thought, *Finally I'm getting this down—I know what it takes, and I'll pull it off. God will be pleased with me, and it'll probably help me to do well in my work.*

Then one day the young man's life began to come apart. Walking into the restaurant of a downtown hotel, he found his wife sitting in an out-of-the-way booth with the curator of the museum where she had been putting in so many volunteer hours. When he challenged her about the encounter later that evening, she tearfully admitted that she was having an affair.

He was devastated.

When he asked her why, she simply said, "You don't seem interested in me anymore. You're wrapped up in your work and in your toys—your car, your boat. I was wrong to let it happen, and I feel horrible about it—but he made me feel important, alive, needed. I just didn't consider the consequences."

"You of all people—how could you do this to me?" he yelled.

"I didn't think you would care!" she shouted back. "I haven't felt that you cared about me for a long time. All you've been interested in is getting ahead and getting more things. There's got to be more to life—to our relationship—than that. I was wrong to get involved with someone else, but things have to change. They just can't keep going like they are."

The young man was shocked. He wasn't sure what to do. That night he didn't go to bed. Sitting at the desk in his upstairs study, his mind went over and over the events of his life. *I've got to find something to help me put this thing back together*, he thought. *Here I am. Everybody thinks I'm successful—that I have it all. And I'm not even sure my wife wants to stay with me.*

Rummaging through a stack of mail on his desk, he came across a flier he had received in the mail the previous week. It was an invitation to attend a seminar being conducted by the author of a book titled *The One Minute Christian*. The seminar was called "Managing Your Life." As he looked at the ad, the young man became excited. "Hey, maybe this is what I need," he exclaimed. "Maybe this guy's seminar can help me put it back together spiritually. I sure need something."

Then the man noticed the dates of the seminar, and his enthusiasm deflated. It had been held the previous week-end. Undaunted, however, he made up his mind. *I gotta go see this guy. I'm sure he's busy. But if he'll give me some time to talk with him, maybe I can get to the heart of what he's talking about—get my life back together.*

Having made up his mind, the young man lay down on the couch in his study and promptly fell asleep.

The next morning things were tense between the young man and his wife. Neither had much to say. The previous night both had raised their voices in anger. Now, in the light of day, the young man told his wife, "Listen, I've made a decision. I'm going to see this guy—I think he's called the One Minute Christian. He does those seminars. You remember the thing we got in the mail a few weeks ago?"

"Wasn't his seminar last weekend?" the man's wife asked.

"Yeah, I missed it. But I'm going to try to get in touch with his office—see if I can set up an appointment with him. I gotta talk to somebody. Maybe he can help."

Later that morning at the office, the young man took time from his responsibilities to phone the number on the flyer. He discovered that the author lived in a nearby city— less than an hour away. Placing a call to the author's secretary, he asked if it would be possible to set up an appointment with the author himself. He was delighted to learn that he would be able to see the man the very next day.

The rest of that day, the young man tried to work—but his heart and mind just weren't in it. He kept going over and over the events of the previous twenty-four hours. *How could she do this to me?* But then he wondered, *How could I do this to* her? *Life's great. We have it all. How could we mess things up so badly?*

Finally, the young man picked up his telephone, dialed his boss's extension, and made arrangements to take a personal day from his schedule. He finished the afternoon by delegating several projects to his secretary and to a couple of colleagues. He left the office early, retrieved his platinum BMW from the parking garage, and headed for home.

The following morning the young man dressed in his favorite suit—an Armani—and a conservative maroon paisley tie. He checked the Rolex watch on his left wrist, gulped down another cup of coffee, then headed out earlier than usual. Fighting rush hour traffic from two cities, it took the young man more than an hour to near the place of his appointment. Finally, the traffic began to thin. It was all he could do to hold his car near the speed limit, thinking, *Maybe I'm about to get some answers.*

Almost before the two men had exchanged greetings, the young man blurted out, "So you're the One Minute Christian. I think you have what I've been looking for."

Following the directions he had obtained from the secretary the previous day, he arrived at a rather ordinary-looking office across the street from an elementary school and near a tree-shaded, middle-class neighborhood. As he walked through the door, he felt a burst of optimism. *Maybe this guy can help me turn my life around. After all, things have to get better.*

After offering him a fresh cup of coffee, the secretary ushered him into a somewhat cluttered office. Sitting behind a desk surrounded by bookcases was a rather nondescript man of average build and height. His thinning hair was somewhat mussed. His blue eyes sparkled, and he broke into a smile as he offered a firm handshake.

In one corner of the office stood a scarred conference table, complete with old-style, leather, high-backed chairs. On the wall near the table hung a white acrylic marker-board. Across the room, tan drapes covered the window.

Almost before the two men had exchanged greetings, the young man blurted out, "So you're the One Minute Christian. I think you have what I've been looking for."

The older man interrupted, his hands raised defensively. "Whoa, hold on. I don't call myself the One Minute Christian. But, here, have a seat. Let's talk about it."

After what seemed to the young man like an extremely long pause, the older man finally broke the ice. "So you read my book?"

The young man quickly replied, "Well—to tell the truth —no."

"So what brought you to me?"

"Actually—I'm not sure. Forty-eight hours ago I thought everything was great. I figured my life was pretty well wired together. I have a great job, more money than I can spend, and an investment account that's handled by one of the top money managers in the country—I know because I'm a money manager myself. I oversee several institutional investment accounts, and I'm doing very well. But things are falling apart, and I'm really not sure why."

The older man leaned back in his chair, sipped his coffee, and set the cup down on the conference table beside him. "So you haven't read the book. I guess I'm a little puzzled. How did you get my name?"

The young man bolted from his chair, almost spilling his coffee. Then he began pacing the floor of the office. "You see, it's like this. I don't really know how to say it, but I found out that my wife has been, you know, involved with somebody else."

The young man tugged at his collar in discomfort. "It came as quite a shock. We've been going to church together. We have a great life, lots of nice things, clothes—you name it. I have a super job. Everything seemed perfect—till now. Now I just feel hollow inside, like none of that matters anymore.

"Anyway, I was sitting in my study last night, and I ran across a flier I had seen for the seminar you did this past week in our city. I pulled it out, read the blurb about *The One Minute Christian,* and decided maybe you had something that could help me.

"You see, I'm an action-oriented person. I believe in trying to figure out what to do about something—and going for it. A few years ago, right after I got my degree, I started working for a successful corporation. I continued reading books, attended seminars, and applied some of the principles I learned. I think that's a big factor in my becoming the youngest vice president in our firm's history. It's also a big part of why I'll probably make $150,000 this coming year— maybe more, with my bonus. By the way, I'll be glad to pay you for your time."

The older man smiled, "I'm not a professional counselor—I don't charge for my time. I speak at seminars, I write, and I take time to talk to people. Now, to be candid with you, since you haven't read the book, what you don't know is that *The One Minute Christian* doesn't contain any deep, revolutionary, ultra-quick, super-spiritual secrets. In fact, what I present in the book is a summary of basic principles taught by men and women who've known God well and who've passed on their knowledge. It's very basic stuff."

As he listened to his host, the young man became skeptical. *Oh boy, what can this guy tell me? He's probably never been a success in business. Maybe I've come to the wrong place.*

Disappointment clouding his face, the young man responded, "I read the blurb on the back of your book. It talked about Christianity for the nineties. One of the reviewer's said, 'Nobody's ever written anything like *The One Minute Christian.*' But now you're telling me your book doesn't have any super-secret shortcuts?"

"That's correct. I'm convinced there aren't any. Now I know that when you're used to living life in the fast lane, you need all the super-quick help you can get. But there are some things that just can't be microwaved. And faith is one of them."

Pausing for a moment, the older man decided to make his young visitor an offer. "I know without even asking that you're a very busy man. But I sense you'd really like to upgrade your spiritual life."

The young man's face brightened. "*Upgrade*. Yes, that's the term. I think that describes exactly what I'd like to do with the spiritual part of my life, my relationships, and everything."

He paused thoughtfully. "You know, I'm a frequent flyer on one of the major airlines. In fact, my company requires me to visit several of its branches to oversee new computer trading programs. Whenever possible I try to upgrade my seat to first class. Yes. That's what I'd like to do—upgrade my spiritual life. Become a first-class Christian."

The older man smiled. "Well, it doesn't quite work that way. God doesn't provide bonus points or premiums in the Christian life. But there *are* some basic principles. Tell you what I'll do. If you'd be willing to carve the time out of your busy schedule to get together with me once a week, I'll take the time to go over some of the basic principles I've included in *The One Minute Christian.*"

"When can we start?" the young man eagerly asked. "I'm ready to get going yesterday!"

He was surprised at the reply. "What about today?"

"Can you spare the time? Isn't your schedule booked?"

"No problem. If you're free, I'll *make* the time."

The older man picked up the telephone, requested that his secretary reschedule a couple things, then leaned back in his chair. "Are you ready?"

"I sure am! Hit me with an earthshaking principle."

With a twinkle in his eye, the older man rose from his chair and moved to the arrangement of bookcases in the corner of his office. He pointed to a plaque on the top shelf of the bookcase. It was inscribed with five large symbols:

1   D   A   A   T

1

LIVING ONE DAY AT A TIME

What's that mean?" the young man asked, as he removed a Mont Blanc pen from his shirt pocket and a wallet-sized, calfskin notebook from his coat. He held his pen poised above the notebook.

"Wait," the older man replied. "Don't write anything down yet. Let's just talk."

The young man placed his expensive writing instrument on the conference table. Then he was shocked—even disappointed—as he watched his mentor-to-be pick up a red-tipped felt marker and write on the acrylic board, "Principle 1: Live one day at a time."

"This is confusing," the young man responded. "'Live one day at a time?' I've attended seminars, read books, and listened to radio and television sermons. Some of them have talked about the sweet by-and-by. Many of them have discussed planning for the future, prioritizing, goal-setting. Now you're telling me to live life one day at a time."

Inwardly the young man was saying, *This guy's so simplistic! How can such a dumb slogan be of any help? Oh, well. I'll hear him out—at least this time.*

"There was a time," the older man continued, "when I was as concerned as you are about living as productively and effectively as possible. I wanted to achieve a lot, especially in my Christian life. In fact, I remember hearing preachers in the church where I grew up challenge us to 'burn out' rather than 'rust out' for God. You know what? I almost did just that—burn out."

Nodding briskly, the young man interrupted. "That's how I feel right now—sort of burned out. I've been working so hard at trying to become a first-class person and trying to succeed at my job at the same time. I've even told my wife about feeling burned out. She's been quite concerned about me, even with what's been going on in her own life. She's told me she feels that a lot of the time when I'm with her I'm not really there. I'm either worrying about things back at the office, or I'm thinking about something else."

The older man smiled as though remembering something. Then he returned to his chair and sat down. "I can relate to that. I used to be the same way—until I met a man named Gil Phillips. If you're in the investment business, you may have heard of him. The Phillips Companies. Phillips Construction, Phillips Properties?"

"Hey, I have!" the young man exclaimed. "He's one of my boss's top clients. I met him in the office a few weeks ago. So how did *you* meet him?"

"Well, I was involved in a struggling enterprise. A mutual friend introduced us. We became very close friends. Began getting together for lunch on a fairly regular basis. He told me the story about Phillips Enterprises. Ever heard it?"

"Wherever you are, be all there.
Live to the hilt each day what
you believe to be the will of God."

"No I haven't—but Gil Phillips is a man whose reputation I'm quite familiar with. Everybody who knows him calls him a success."

"Let me tell you what I learned from him." Leaning back in his chair, he pulled the cord to open his drapes, then looked out the window of his office. Reflected sunshine sparkled from the windshields of moving vehicles. An older couple walked past on the sidewalk beneath, the man pushing a small shopping cart. Muted laughter could be heard, the sounds of children playing in the nearby school yard.

Crossing his legs, the older man continued. "Gil Phillips inherited a small chain of grocery stores from his dad—a hard-working, self-made man who died of a heart attack at an early age. They also owned a struggling insurance agency, a cleaners, and a 'five and dime.' But his dad was focused—boy was he focused! Gil, on the other hand, was sort of interested in all kinds of different activities. The family business, plus about fifteen other things. Gil's dad, to hear him tell it, didn't think he'd ever amount to much of anything. But his dad gave him a motto—something he'd read in a book somewhere that really changed his life—and Gil's."

Leaning forward the young man asked, "How could a motto change a person's life?"

"Good question, but this one did."

"What was it?"

The older man looked at the ceiling and began to recite. "Wherever you are, be all there. Live to the hilt each day what you believe to be the will of God."

"That's catchy. 'Wherever you are, be all there.' It says exactly what I haven't been much of lately. I've been worrying about my future at work—what I'm going to do to keep my career track moving ahead. I've even been concerned about what to incorporate into my religious life to improve it. I'll admit, I hadn't been giving much thought to being a successful husband—I thought I was doing a pretty good job at that. But I must not have been doing as well as I thought—" The young man's voice trailed off.

The older man stretched and leaned back in his chair. "What you told me about your marriage—I know it must be painful for you. But I think I learned from Gil Phillips what he learned from his dad—or from whoever came up with it originally—to live life a day at a time, one situation at a time—even one minute at a time.

"That's been a hard lesson for me to learn. I keep finding myself worrying about the future. What if this happens?

What if that occurred? What if I don't succeed? Or, if I wasn't worried about the future, I'd be going over and over the mistakes of the past. Why didn't I do so-and-so? How could I have forgotten? Living one day at a time, one minute at a time—it's been hard for me to learn. But I *have* learned it—and it works."

"So now you've got this business of living one minute at a time down pretty well, huh? That must be why you're the One Minute Christian."

The older man held up his hand in protest. "Well, I'm not sure I have this lesson down pat yet. And I really wouldn't call myself the One Minute Christian."

Grinning, the young man replied, "I think that's what I'd like to call you—the One Minute Christian."

"Well, that's OK, I guess—as long as you get my point. Especially after what's happened in your life, I think it's going to be crucial for you to learn to start living one day at a time, even one situation at a time. Gil Phillips learned that's how he had to start operating in his life.

"It all started for Gil when disaster struck one day. A flood wiped out the most successful of their stores—and they were extremely underinsured. Gil told me how vividly he remembered driving through the recently flooded streets of the neighborhood. While they looked at the wreckage, his dad came up with an idea. 'All these people are going to need to rebuild. We've been trying to manage several different kinds of businesses, none of them very successfully.'

"So Gil and his dad started a construction company. They helped the people whose homes had been flooded to rebuild. They hired men who were out of work—and there were plenty of people out of work back then—and the rest is history. Eventually they became large enough to get into investments, real estate—those kinds of activities. But they never stopped construction—and they never stopped concentrating on the main thing. Gil said they made 'Wherever you are, be all there' their official motto. And he passed that motto on to me.

"At the time, my life was like the idealistic Western hero who jumped on his horse and tried to ride off in all directions at once. Gil Phillips challenged me to start living one day—one situation—at a time. In fact, he told me that's how Jesus operated in *His* life.

"What do you mean?" the young man asked.

"Ever hear of the Sermon on the Mount?"

"Sure, but I don't remember much about it."

"That's where Jesus first announced His offer of the kingdom of heaven. It's the point at which He told the religious leaders of His day that they weren't good enough for the kingdom. And He explained to His followers how to live as part of His kingdom."

"Sounds like something *we* could use," the young man replied.

"Exactly. So let's take a look it."

Pulling a Bible from the bookshelf to his right, he flipped through several pages, found what he was looking for, then handed the book to the young man. Putting his finger in the upper left-hand corner of the page, he said, "Read this."

The young man began to read: "'So don't be anxious about tomorrow. God will take care of your tomorrow too. Live one day at a time.' Hey, there's that 'one day at a time' motto. But what does He mean by telling us not to be anxious about tomorrow? It sounds like He's saying not even to worry about what's going to happen tomorrow."

"That's exactly what He's getting at. Now He's not telling us never to plan for the future. He's just warning us against becoming unduly distracted, concerned, or worried. In fact, the word He used—the word that means *be anxious*—that's a term that actually means to be divided or distracted in your mind."

"'Divided or distracted'? I'm not sure I understand. Do you mean we're not supposed to let what *might* happen tomorrow distract us from what is happening today?"

The older man smiled. "You're on the right track. What

Jesus is saying is, Don't become distracted from the major purpose of life by trying to make a living or meeting your financial obligations. People in Jesus' day were probably as concerned about material things as we are today."

As the young man thought about his own pocket full of credit cards—platinum and gold—plus his recession-shrunken portfolio and the mounting stack of bills on his desk at home, he shook his head. "I doubt it."

"Look at this verse," responded his mentor. "'So don't worry at all about having enough food and clothing. Why be like the heathen?' That means we shouldn't make the necessities of life what we worry about, what we pour our lives into. That should not be our top priority."

Remembering what he had been told in the classroom as he pursued his MBA, the young man said, "Are you telling me that being a Christian is supposed to be more important than my job? More important than making a living? That sounds a bit radical."

I should've figured this guy would try to separate me from my money. Now he's probably going to tell me that Jesus wants me to get rid of everything I have and take a vow of poverty, like a monk. With a sarcastic note in his voice he asked, "What exactly are you trying to tell me—get rid of my possessions?"

The older man responded gently, "*I* don't want to tell you anything. Why don't you take a look at what *Jesus* says?" Putting his finger on the page in front of the young man, he said, "Read this."

The young man almost couldn't believe what he was seeing. Quietly he read the words "'But your heavenly Father already knows perfectly well that you need them, and he will give them to you if you give him first place in your life and live as he wants you to.' So He's not telling me I have to get rid of my car, my house—even my credit cards?"

"Not hardly. I think the major issue is not what we have or don't have—it's our attitude about it. It's what we consider to be really important."

Reaching into his pocket, he took out a worn 3x5 card, held it up to the light as he examined it, then passed it to the young man.

"It's the same thing you just read—just in a different version of the Bible. I wanted you to see this because there are two words Jesus mentions that explain what it means to give Him first place in your life and live as He wants you to live.

The young man took the card. Silently his lips formed the words. "But seek first the kingdom of God and His righteousness, and all these things shall be added to you" (NKJV). The young man couldn't help noticing that the words *kingdom* and *righteousness* had been heavily underlined with a felt tip marker.

"God's kingdom and righteousness—I'm not sure that computes for me." The young man smiled, somewhat sheepishly. "I guess I'm more into democracies than kingdoms."

The older man smiled in response. "I think I understand what you mean. When Jesus spoke of His kingdom, part of what He meant was that He has a right to be in charge, like a king. In other words, He has the right to be the final authority in our lives. After all, kings have the final say in their kingdoms."

He pointed to the book in front of the young man. "It's exactly what you just read. 'And he will give them to you if you give him first place in your life.'"

"And 'His righteousness' is living as He wants you to?" the young man asked.

"Precisely. *Righteousness* is just a word that refers to a right standard of living—doing what's right, as opposed to what's wrong."

"Sounds pretty simple."

"It is. Unfortunately, we haven't always sought His righteousness, or lived as He wants us to—at least I haven't."

"No," the young man responded, "I'm not perfect either. In fact, I've never met anyone who was. Maybe it's time I tried this business of living one day at a time."

Leaning back in his seat, the young man looked intently at the man who had now become his mentor. He noticed the man's ruddy complexion, his face lined with wrinkles.

"As you said, Jesus told us to live one day at a time. You told me you learned about it from Gil Phillips who evidently practiced it. Anybody else make it work?"

"Sure. Hal Harris, for one."

The young man's mouth dropped open in surprise. "Hal Harris Seminars? *That* Hal Harris? Why he's one of the all-time heroes of the business world. One of America's top motivational speakers. The guy's a legend in corporate America. Why, the *Wall Street Journal* even profiled him. I've never attended one of his seminars, but I'm planning to one of these days."

The older man leaned back in his chair. "A couple years ago, I had the opportunity to attend one. Now, when they conduct these seminars—they last several days, you know—Hal and the members of his staff cover everything you could possibly want to know about management, motivating people, selling, you name it.

"But what I remember most was the last evening. Hal was winding up the final session, building to a climax. Then he dropped this bombshell on us. Said something like this, 'After this session, the seminar will be over. You're free to go. But if any of you would like to stay behind and learn what really makes me tick, find out my personal philosophy of life, I'd be glad for you to do so. Now it's gonna be late— we'll finish here about 10:00 P.M., and I'll start the optional session at about 11:00. It'll take me thirty or forty minutes. You certainly aren't obligated to stay—my feelings won't be hurt. But you're welcome to stay if you want to. Just don't feel any pressure to do so."

"So let me guess," the young man responded. "Nobody stayed but you and one other person."

"That's what I expected. But, actually, almost half the people who were attending the seminar crowded into that little room—it was one of the side rooms where they held some of the breakout sessions.

"What amazed me is that Hal basically attributed all his success to one factor in his life—Jesus Christ. Said that he decided years ago to give Jesus Christ first place in his life, and he's never regretted it. He says that every day before he does anything else he talks to the Lord in a private kind of devotional time. Then, during the remainder of the day, he frequently consults with the Lord."

"That's hokey," the young man interrupted. "How can he consult with the Lord? Does he carry some kind of a pocket phone with a direct line to heaven or something?"

"No. I remember he talked about Moses—you know, the guy who parted the waters of the Red Sea? He said he had made Moses one of his role models, could really identify with a man who turned down the opportunity to be the CEO of the mightiest nation on earth at that time—Egypt. Said Moses chose to identify with God's people instead."

"How could some obscure guy from centuries ago who lived in the Middle East be the driving force behind one of the top business leaders in America today? It just doesn't make sense."

"One of the lessons I've learned from years of being a Christian is that God is with me every minute of every day—not just today. That's why I can live one day at a time."

"Well, it made sense to me," the older man responded. "The main reason is a statement about Moses from another part of the Bible—I have it right here." Picking up another 3x5 card—which showed evidence of being handled numerous times—the older man handed it to his young friend.

"This quote comes from a place in the Bible called 'the faith chapter,' where it talks about a number of people who learned to live by faith—by depending on God. Moses was one of them."

The young man bent over the card and looked at it closely. "By faith he forsook Egypt, not fearing the wrath of the king; for he endured as seeing Him who is invisible" (NKJV).

Looking up at his mentor, the young man inquired, "What's this all about? I still don't get it."

"Just think about it for a minute. Who would be invisible to Moses?"

"God, I guess."

"Exactly."

"But does that mean Moses actually saw Him? You know, I used to wonder a lot about what God actually looks like. Sort of thought of him as an old man with a long beard, or maybe somebody wearing a robe the way our minister used to when I was growing up."

The older man replied thoughtfully, "There were times when Moses was given a glimpse of God's glory. But this isn't talking about some spectacular experience like that. I believe what's being said is that Moses endured all the daily difficulties of life because he lived as though God were walking through them right beside him. He persisted in life, a day at a time, considering God to be right with him. Here, let me show you what it says in this Bible."

He flipped some pages and handed the Bible to the young man with his finger on the verse. It read, "Moses kept right on going; it seemed as though he could see God right there with him."

With a sweeping gesture, the old man asked, "Who are the occupants of this room?"

Without hesitation the young man replied, "Why, you and I, of course." Pausing a moment he added, "And God?"

"How do you know?" the older man asked with just a trace of a smile on his face.

The young man stretched his arms above his head for a minute and looked out the window. Then he refocused his attention on his companion. "I think I see what you're getting at. But I'm still not sure it makes sense. Moses couldn't see God on a day-in, day-out basis, but God was real to him. Is that your point?"

"Exactly. And according to Hal Harris, Moses was the role model for his own daily walk with God."

The young man's retort was quick. "And is that how it is in your life?"

"That's how it came to be. Now, I don't get up in the morning and see God the way I see my wife across from me at the breakfast table. I don't pass him at the corner on the way to the office or run into him in the coffee shop where I eat lunch. But he's right with me every step of the way. One of the lessons I've learned from years of being a Christian is that God is with me every minute of every day—not just today. That's why I can live one day at a time."

"We're back to a One Minute Christianity?" the young man replied sarcastically. "I still have trouble swallowing that—even if somebody as successful as Hal Harris is selling it. But I'll try to keep an open mind."

"It might be better to call it 'minute-to-minute Christianity'—or 'experience-to-experience.' You've been through some pretty tough experiences lately, haven't you? Ever felt like giving up?"

"Every day," the young man acknowledged without hesitation.

His mentor picked up the copy of the Bible, turned some pages, and pointed. "Look what the apostle Paul wrote. He was a man who learned that this business worked. He was in the middle of one of the most trying experiences anyone ever went through. In fact, after what you found out about your wife, you probably felt about like Paul did. Paul's problem wasn't marriage—although there's a good chance he had been married and his marriage had broken up when he stopped being a Pharisee and became a Christian. No, that wasn't Paul's problem.

"You see, Paul had been persecuted intensely because of his faith in Jesus Christ. Right here it says he was surrounded by trouble—but he didn't give up. He was discouraged, but not in despair. He felt like he was being pursued, but he knew God hadn't abandoned him. Life had thrown him down, tripped him up—but he wasn't destroyed."

After staring at the page before him intently for a moment, the young man replied, "Seems like I remember hearing in church about Paul's being in a shipwreck once and being beaten. Did I hear right? And did he actually have to escape from some city by being let down in a basket from the wall?"

"He went through all that—and quite a bit more. But he never gave up." Pointing to the page before him, he began to read. "That is why we never give up. Though our bodies are dying, our inner strength in the Lord is growing every day."

Placing a hand on the young man's shoulder, he looked at him intently and asked, "Did you notice those last three words—'growing every day'?"

"One day at a time, eh?" the young man observed wryly.

"Exactly. That's Paul's way of putting it. One day at a time. On the outside, life was falling apart. Circumstances looked grim, he didn't feel so hot physically, and it seems he had been abandoned by most of his friends. But he never gave up. And the reason he didn't is simple. He had learned the secret of living one day at a time."

With a somewhat puzzled look on his face, the young man replied, "I'm still not sure how this all relates to me. I mean, some parts of my life are going really well—like my work. Others, my marriage for instance, aren't very good at all."

"That's why I'd encourage you and your wife to begin seeing a marriage counselor—I know a good one whose office is not too far from you. I recommend him highly. I'll get his phone number for you from my secretary before you leave. What I want to do is help you pick up some practical things that can make a difference in the parts of your life that are going well—not to mention those that aren't."

Walking across the office to his markerboard, the older man wrote the numbers one, two, and three in a vertical line. "Here are a few implications of this principle, some ways it touches your life and mine.

Beside the first number he wrote the word "Trust."

"First, I trust God for each day's needs—that day. Did you grow up in a church where they said The Lord's Prayer every Sunday?"

With a satisfied smile, the young man replied, "Yes, I did. It was part of the ritual. Never did figure out what it was all about. But we said it every week, whether we needed to or not."

"Well," the older man continued, "one line in the prayer says, 'Give us our food day by day,' or, as the liturgy has it, 'Give us this day our daily bread.' So Jesus is actually telling us to rely on Him for—and even pray about—our basic, daily needs. Can you think of anything you need today?"

The young man paused in thought. "I need to know what to do about my marriage. I guess I really want it to work. I think I'm probably more upset with myself than I am with my wife. But I'm pretty angry at her too."

"A lot of us tend to pick up our concept of what God is like from our human fathers."

"I'm sure there are a lot of feelings to work out between the two of you, a lot of things that need to happen to rebuild trust. Maybe what you really need is wisdom. There's a place in the Bible where James the brother of Jesus says that, if anyone lacks wisdom, let him ask of God who gives freely, no strings attached, and it will be given to him. So you need wisdom, and you probably need strength to handle this crisis. Ask God for that as well."

"Sounds like I have a lot to pray about. Do you really think God has time to listen to me whine about all my problems?"

His private answer to that question was, *There's no way God's going to have time to fool around with this kind of penny-ante stuff. There are more than five billion people on this planet. Even Dad didn't have time to listen to my problems.*

The young man was jolted back to the present when a fragment of what the older man was saying pierced his reverie. ". . . You've picked up a lot of what you think about God from your earthly father. Was your dad the sort of person who didn't have a lot of time to waste listening to your problems?"

"How—how did you guess?" the young man replied, feeling strangely naked before an apparent mind reader.

"Seems like a lot of us were raised in homes where one or both of our parents didn't have time for us. My dad used to tell me, 'Son, you need to become a self-made man. You need to get to the place where you don't have to ask anybody for anything.'"

The young man nodded vigorously. "That's the way my dad was. Said his dad had taught him to be that way too."

"There's the problem. A lot of us tend to pick up our concept of what God is like from our human fathers. That would be fine—except few dads measure up to the kind of loving involvement God has. You see, I've learned from years as a Christian that God is a perfect Father. He never turns me away when I come to Him with a need. He doesn't love me based on how well I perform. And if He didn't intend for me to come to Him about my daily needs, He wouldn't have told me so. Now, the look on your face tells me that this is still sort of hard for you to take—but give it a try."

Turning back to the markerboard, he wrote "Present" beside the second number.

"Here's a second implication of this principle of living one day at a time. I need to quit living in the past—or for that matter in the future. I may remember the past—in fact, I will, since our past experiences have been recorded indelibly in the brain. I may anticipate the future, even pray about events to come. But the major focus of my life is today, with its problems, its hassles. For example, what would you consider to be your biggest problem right now?"

"My marriage, without question," the young man replied.

"I agree. That's probably where you need to concentrate right now. But you can't rebuild everything immediately. It's a one-day-at-a-time proposition.

Beside the third number on the board he wrote the words "Don't Quit."

"And that brings me to a third application of this principle. No matter how bad any one day seems, don't give up. Like Jesus said, 'God will take care of your tomorrow too. Live one day at a time.' At times the apostle Paul actually feared for his life, but he didn't quit. After all, even the worst of days only last twenty-four hours."

The young man grimaced as he thought, *Boy, I've just been through a couple of the worst I've ever had.* Out loud he said, "Yeah, I can relate. I feel like a line someone used in a story at a management seminar I attended. 'Cheer up, things could be worse. So I cheered up, and sure enough— they got worse.'"

"It's certainly hard to consider some things to be any good," the older man replied. "At least they're like what I heard an old preacher say years ago. They 'come to pass and not to stay.'"

The older man glanced at his watch. The young man noticed it was a Timex rather than a Rolex. "We're out of time for today. But I want you to see one more thing about this business of living a day at a time. It takes balance."

"Balance?"

"Right. Balance between facing each day's circumstances and problems and living in light of what is eternal. That's what this statement by Paul is about. Let me read it.

These troubles and sufferings of ours are, after all, quite small and won't last very long. Yet this short time of distress will result in God's richest blessing upon us forever and ever! So we do not look at what we can see right now, the troubles all around us; but we look forward to the joys in heaven which we have not yet seen. The troubles will soon be over, but the joys to come will last forever.

The older man closed his copy of Scripture and balanced it on his right index finger. "Most of us have a lot of trouble with balance. We either get so wrapped up in the problems of today we lose sight of what is eternal, or we're like some Christians I've known who were so heavenly minded they were of no earthly good—everything that matters is in the 'sweet by-and-by.'

"I think we have to face what comes at us day by day— but we face it by looking through it and beyond it to the fact that this life is just preparation for the next. I suspect *you've* been concentrating on the present—especially your work— and neglecting the priority of what's eternal. But we'll talk more about that in the days ahead. Then I think you'll see what I'm getting at."

I'm not so sure, the young man thought. *This guy has some good things to say, but I don't want to go head over heels about this stuff. After all, he's been around a lot longer than I have, but his net worth is probably nowhere near what mine is already.*

"So I guess I'm signed on for a crash course with the One Minute Christian," he said aloud to his older companion.

"I guess you could put it that way. What time can you come next week?"

2

LIVING BITTER FREE

The following week, the young man was eager to continue his interaction with the man he had begun referring to as the One Minute Christian. He arranged his schedule so he could leave his office early in the afternoon. Since he was going in the opposite direction from rush hour traffic, he was able to get to the older man's office more quickly than the previous week.

Unfortunately, he wasn't in a very good frame of mind. In fact, as he drove toward the older man's office, he found himself feeling more and more upset. His mind kept replaying the scene in the coffee shop of the hotel, where he had found his wife with the museum curator. Every time he thought about it, he felt sick to his stomach.

"How could she have done this to me?" he forced through gritted teeth. "Sure I didn't pay much attention to her, but I didn't deserve this." He didn't think he could ever trust her again.

And that jerk from the museum. I'd like to rearrange his face with a baseball bat!

As a car cut into the lane in front of him, he angrily honked his horn. The man reminded him of his boss, and that brought back memories of the conflict he'd had in a meeting that morning. *I can't believe he'd embarrass me like that—and in front of the other vice presidents.*

As he pulled his BMW into the parking lot at the office of his mentor, the young man determined to put his negative feelings behind him. He forced a smile on his face and walked briskly into the foyer of the older man's office. At the invitation of the man's secretary, Debra Lee, he marched into his mentor's office, accepted the warm handshake and fresh cup of coffee, and took the proffered seat.

To his surprise, the older man almost immediately asked, "What's bothering you today?"

"Nothing," he quickly replied.

Looking intently at him, the older man raised his eyebrows. "Are you sure? I really expect you to be honest with me."

This guy must *be a mind reader!* the young man thought. *I just hope he doesn't drag up this thing with my wife. I don't think I can handle it today.*

He hesitated, then replied, "It's my boss. We had another run-in in a meeting this morning—he humiliated me in front of the other vice presidents. The guy is impossible at times! He expects me to bend steel in my bare hands, leap the office building in a single bound, and change clothes in a phone booth."

The older man grinned. "I remember when people thought *pastors* were supermen. Some people still do."

"Were you a pastor?" the young man asked with a puzzled look on his face.

"For quite some time, when I was younger. That's how I got started doing seminars on One Minute Christianity."

"So you weren't always the One Minute Christian. Well, you certainly don't remind me of any pastors *I* know—that's a compliment by the way." To himself he said, *No wonder I feel like he's preaching at me sometimes.*

The older man walked behind his desk and pulled the curtains back. Dark clouds covered the sky. It looked like heavy rain could begin at any minute.

"Is the sun shining?" the older man asked.

"What do you mean? It's cloudy, and it's probably going to start pouring before I leave here."

"But is the sun shining?"

"Sure, I suppose it is. But you can't see it through the clouds."

"Sounds like where you are right now. Maybe the sun is shining in your life, but perhaps this conflict at work has cast a cloud over things."

The young man shrugged.

"I know you probably don't feel like talking about it, but I can't help wondering if what happened with your wife is part of the problem."

Quickly, the young man replied, "I don't think so. Besides, I'd rather not talk about that today. I guess we'll see a counselor—eventually. In fact, I plan to call that counselor you told me about this week. But I thought I'd try to do things one step at a time—like you suggested last time."

"You're sure you don't want to talk about your feelings about that?"

The young man buried his face in his hands. It was all he could do to keep from bursting into tears. *What's wrong with me? I'm losing control. I can't let this guy see me like this!*

The older man was still standing at the window, watching the movement of the clouds. "You know," he said, "clouds eventually blow away. But sometimes things get worse before they get better."

"Thanks for the encouragement," the young man replied thickly.

Unperturbed, the older man walked away from the window and sat down in the chair next to his young visitor. "In the normal course of things, clouds blow in. Sometimes it rains, even storms. But usually, pretty quickly, the clouds roll away. Can you imagine what things would be like if it stayed cloudy for months at a time?

"That's how things are in the lives of some people. I'd like to share some things with you about one of life's greatest risks—one that can cloud any life. For somebody whose been hit with what you've just experienced in your marriage, it's a pretty serious risk. I'm referring to the danger of bitterness."

The older man paused for a moment, and his young visitor quizzically responded, "Bitterness? Sounds like my

Aunt Sally. She's as bitter as a lemon—or a bowl of sauer-kraut. Last Christmas, our whole family got together for the first time in years. We were all looking forward to a great time, but she single-handedly ruined things for everybody. Nobody can hardly stand to visit her any more."

"Do you think *you're* ever bitter?"

Quickly the young man replied, "Of course not." But he thought, *He's going to start reading my mind again.* After a pause he said, "Well, I don't think so. But I'm not too sure right now."

"Intense, underlying anger presents the greatest health hazard to Type As."

The old man's words were kind but firm. "What about this thing with your wife—and the guy she was involved with. You don't suppose you might be holding a grudge against her—or him? And what about your boss?"

"Maybe," the young man conceded. "But if you'd been through what I have, you'd probably be holding some grudges too. In fact, doesn't the Bible say 'vengeance is mine'? Maybe God wants me to get even with this guy for wrecking my marriage."

"I can certainly understand your feelings. But maybe we need to talk about what bitterness is and who it really hurts." Walking over to the markerboard in the corner of his office, he uncapped a green pen. Then he wrote a single word in large, messy letters:

A N G E R

He exchanged the green pen for a red one, drew several bold circles around the word he had written, then turned to his friend. "Ever get this way?"

"Sure. I guess I've been that way a lot of the time recently, even before this business came up with my wife. She's been on my case a lot about being a Type A personality."

"Do you think you are? Type A, that is?"

"Probably so. Most successful people are, aren't they? So what?"

"I did some reading this past week," the older man replied gently. "I discovered that most Type As are in a hurry. That's probably not a surprise to you."

"No. I spend most of my time in the fast lane, whether I'm driving or not."

Picking up his visitor's humor, the older man grinned pleasantly. "There's another component to Type A—anger. It's one of the major characteristics of Type A people. In fact, the article I read suggests that intense, underlying anger presents the greatest health hazard to Type As."

"Hmm. I always figured the main thing about Type As was that they were just in a hurry and were more likely to become traffic casualties."

"Well, I guess that is a danger, but from what I read the danger of a heart attack or a stroke as a result of anger buildup is probably a bigger risk. Let's talk about anger for a minute. Did you ever hear anyone say that it's always a sin to be angry?"

"When I was a kid, my mother used to tell me that a lot."

"Guess what? I used to hear a lot of the same thing. But your mother was wrong."

"I don't think so," the young man said. "I think *you're* wrong. I really believe it *is* a sin to be angry."

"Tell you what. I think I can demonstrate to you that anger isn't always sinful. Do you agree with me that Jesus was perfect?"

"I guess so."

"There's pretty strong evidence to back that up," the older man responded. "In fact, at one point, Jesus confronted his bitterest enemies, the Pharisees, with a challenge: 'Which of you can truthfully accuse Me of a single sin?' (John 8:46). They couldn't."

"I don't think I'd dare try something like that," the young man grinned. "My enemies *know* I'm not perfect. So does my wife." He shrugged. "So Jesus was perfect. So what?"

Taking the well-worn copy of Scripture he had used the previous week from his desk, the older man moved to the round conference table in the corner of the office. He invited the young man to join him. Turning to the second gospel in the New Testament—Mark—he pointed at a verse in chapter 3. "Read that," he instructed.

"Looking around at them angrily, for he was deeply disturbed at their indifference to human need, he said to the man, 'Reach out your hand.' He did, and instantly his hand was healed!"

The young man paused, then looked up at his mentor. "That's Jesus isn't it?"

"Right."

"He was perfect, right?"

"Absolutely."

"And He was angry."

"Quite."

"So anger can't always be a sin?"

"Not always."

"I'm still not sure I get what you're driving at," the young man said, "Maybe you better explain this to me further."

"It's like this. Bitterness, as I understand it, is what we might call 'aged anger.' You see, anger is an emotion God has given to us to help protect us. When we are threatened, or good things are threatened—like our marriage—we *ought* to feel angry."

The young man interrupted, "You mean like when children are abused?"

"Exactly! In the verse you just read, Jesus was angry because some of the religious leaders of His day didn't want Him to heal a man with a paralyzed hand, just because of their picky Sabbath regulations. So when someone wrongs us, or even wrongs someone else, and we know about it, anger is a natural emotional response."

"You mean like when my wife—"

"Definitely! When your wife broke the trust in your relationship, the man she was working with took advantage of her emotional vulnerability. He took what was rightfully yours. This morning, when your boss placed unreasonable demands on you, it was natural for you to feel angry. It's also appropriate to share your concerns and feelings with your boss, or your spouse, or whomever you're angry with—as long as you do it in a truthful but kind way."

"I'm not sure I could do that. I'd probably blow them away—at least verbally."

"Well, that's not exactly what I had in mind. You see, we tend to take three typical approaches to anger. One is to stuff it away, let people walk all over us."

"Isn't that the Christian thing to do?" the young man interrupted. "Didn't Jesus say, 'Turn the other cheek?' That's another thing my mother drilled into me when I was a kid."

The older man smiled. "He did say that. But He also said, 'Be as wary as serpents and harmless as doves.'"

Puzzled, the young man scratched his head. "You'll have to explain that one to me."

"Are you telling me it's OK for me to get angry with my boss—or my wife?"

"When I was a kid, I grew up in the country," the older man said. "I used to pick blackberries. Where we lived, we had lots of snakes—they were called copperheads—poisonous little critters. Occasionally someone would be bitten. A few people probably even died from copperhead bites.

"But, usually, if you made enough noise, the snakes would move out of the berry patch ahead of you. In fact, I think those snakes were pretty smart. They always made it a point not to leave their head where you were about to put your foot."

"You mean, they didn't allow themselves to be walked on?" the young man inquired.

"Precisely. I think what Jesus meant about being as wary as serpents was 'Don't let people walk all over you.' Today we call it being assertive."

"But He also said, 'harmless as doves.' How does that fit in?"

"It's just another example of the balance I see in the Bible. Think about it. What does a dove stand for?"

"Peace, I assume. I usually think of hawks as symbolizing war or conflict. They are birds that attack, aren't they?"

"That's what I'm getting at," the older man said. "You just don't think of a dove as attacking. In fact, I suspect it would take something drastic—like disturbing their young —to get a dove to ever attack."

"Are you telling me it's OK for me to get angry with my boss—or my wife?"

"It's not only OK, it's going to happen at times. Getting in touch with feelings of anger is essential for any healthy person. Let me show you another place where the Bible talks about this." Flipping to the book of Ephesians, the older man said, "Take a look at this."

"Kind of hard to read through the notes you've written in your Bible," the young man said.

"Sorry about that. Sometimes I guess I do get carried away."

The young man began reading. "'If you are angry, don't sin by nursing your grudge. Don't let the sun go down with you still angry—get over it quickly.' So how can I get angry and not sin?" the young man asked. "Most of the time when I lose my temper at my wife or really get mad at my boss, I *know* I'm sinning."

The older man walked back to the markerboard in the corner of the room. Picking up a black marker, he drew an arrow from the word *anger*, then wrote another word:

B I T T E R N E S S

He turned to the young man. "Let me explain how anger turns into bitterness. Does anyone take out the garbage at your home?"

"Sure. Usually my wife. Sometimes I do."

"So you do have garbage to take out?"

"Of course. Doesn't everybody?"

"Exactly," the older man said. "And everybody has anger. Now follow me carefully. What do you suppose would happen if you didn't take out the garbage for a month?"

"We'd probably have to move out of the place. I don't think we could stand the smell."

"That's what happens when a person allows bitterness to take over. Remember the last part of the verse you just read?"

"That part about not letting the sun go down on your anger?"

"Yes. The way I see it, that means we need to deal with our anger every day, before we go to bed at night. I've read some psychological studies that indicate that, if we don't, our lives will actually become emotionally poisoned."

"Sounds like my sister. About ten years ago, she was involved in a pretty messy divorce case. You can't hardly get around her without her unloading about her ex-husband. I've tried to tell her not to talk about him in front of her little girl. She keeps on doing it anyway."

The older man continued. "One of the articles I read recently was a research study by a psychologist. It involved a number of couples. The study found that ten years after their divorce half the women and a third of the men were still intensely angry at their former spouses. In fact, that anger had actually poisoned their lives, even affected their relationships with their children."

"Sounds like my sister all right. Her big thing is, she wants to get even. She sort of jokes about it—says things like, 'I've given up trying to get ahead; I just want to get even.' But it sure seems to have made her life miserable."

"That's a pretty good description of bitterness—unresolved anger, combined with the desire to get even. Over the past twenty years I've talked to people from all walks of life. A lot of them are miserable, and most of them felt that way because of bitterness."

Walking back to his chair, the older man asked, "Are you a football fan?"

"You bet!"

"What's your favorite team?"

Without hesitation the young man responded, "The Dallas Cowboys."

"Me too. What a coach that Tom Landry was! Twenty straight winning seasons. Five Super Bowl appearances. Two championships."

"Then he gets dumped by a new owner," the young man interjected. "I still haven't forgiven that guy who bought the Cowboys for firing him. And the way he did it? I swore I'd never buy another ticket to a Cowboys game."

"How do you think Tom Landry feels about what happened?"

"Bitter, I suppose."

Walking to a file cabinet, the older man lifted a manila folder from the "B" section and pulled out a handful of newspaper and magazine clippings. Spreading them over the surface of the conference table, he pointed to one lengthy article. "This is the headline from the sports section of the *Dallas Morning News* the day Tom Landry was fired."

The young man stared at the headline, a look of surprise spreading across his face.

'I'M NOT BITTER' LANDRY SAYS OF FIRING

"I remember that now. Guess I'd forgotten. I read this when it happened. I remember thinking, 'He may not be bitter, but I probably would be.' I just despise the way things happened."

"Yep. He was sixty-four years old, and he said he didn't like the way things happened either. But he refused to hold a grudge."

The older man lifted another piece of paper from the folder. "This is an article from one of the sports magazines. Listen to what this sports writer had to say."

In over twenty years, I got to know Landry as a writer gets to know a coach—never anything more. But I never asked him a question that was not answered honestly. I've written plenty of negative stories about the Cowboys, but not once has he mentioned any of them or shown any resentment.

"That's been years ago," the young man said. "I wonder how he feels now."

Slipping the articles back into the folder, the older man turned to face his young visitor. "I think I can speak to that. Coach Landry puts in some public appearances for an organization I work with. Just a few weeks ago I had a chance to meet with him—finally—one-on-one."

"Wow! A chance to meet Tom Landry! I don't suppose you had a chance to ask him how he felt?"

"Sure did. He admitted he hadn't been happy about the way things happened. In fact, he probably felt just as angry as you or I would have. But he knew he couldn't hold a grudge or let bitterness pull him down. He'd seen how bitterness soured the lives of other people, and he didn't want that to happen to him. So he made up his mind not to hold a grudge. I think that's one reason so many people respect him so highly today."

"Hall of Fame behavior, no doubt about it," the young man responded. "But I'm not sure I could handle some of the raw deals a lot of people have been through."

"Let me tell you about two of the rawest deals I've heard about—one from the Bible and one from recent history. Remember a boy in the book of Genesis by the name of Joseph?"

"Wasn't he the one whose brothers sold him into slavery?"

"That's him. Sold him because they couldn't stand him. Then, when he got down to Egypt, he had more trouble. Because he resisted the sexual advances of his master's wife, he was falsely accused and thrown into prison."

"I'll bet the prisons back then weren't as comfortable as some of those 'country club' prisons they have for white collar criminals today," the young man observed.

His mentor smiled. "No, I suspect it was pretty grim. While in prison Joseph helped one of his fellow prisoners, who later was released. Joseph asked him to put in a good word for him when he got out. But the guy promptly forgot—and Joseph spent two extra years in that prison."

"And he wasn't bitter?"

"Nope. Later, when his brothers came to Egypt looking for food during a famine, Joseph had risen to the number two position in all of Egypt. Of course, his brothers didn't recognize him, but Joseph had no trouble recognizing them. I'm sure he remembered vividly what they had done to him."

"So how come he wasn't bitter? Why didn't he get revenge?"

"He chose a different approach," the older man said. Walking back to his markerboard, he uncapped the green marker and drew a diagonal line through the word *bitterness*. Under it he wrote:

F O R G I V E N E S S

The young man was stunned. *I can't believe this guy. Next thing you know, he's gonna tell me to forgive my wife—and probably the jerk she was involved with too. Fat chance of that happening.*

"So that's where you're headed with this discussion," he noted wryly. "I should have figured. So Joseph forgave his brothers?"

Walking back to the conference table, the older man opened his Bible to the last chapter in the book of Genesis. "Read this," he instructed

The young man began reading where his companion pointed. "'As far as I am concerned, God turned into good what you meant for evil, for he brought me to this high position I have today so that I could save the lives of many people. No, don't be afraid. Indeed, I myself will take care of you and your families.' And he spoke very kindly to them, reassuring them."

Looking up at the older man, the young executive exclaimed, "That's incredible! How could he do that?"

"That's what I've asked myself many times. In fact, last week a young lady named Cindy came in to see me. Her parents had abused her physically and sexually. Her husband was an alcoholic and had beaten her. She had been through a living hell on earth. She told me that for many years she had been bitter. Then one day, something happened that turned her whole life around."

When the older man paused, the young man—as if on cue—asked, "And what was that?"

"Somebody explained to her how much she had been forgiven. When she realized how much she had been forgiven, she found that she could forgive those who had hurt her."

"Wait a minute," the young man interrupted. "Surely she hadn't done anything to anybody that was as bad as what her parents and her husband had done to her."

"Maybe not. But when she realized how much God had forgiven her, she was able to forgive the people against whom she was holding a grudge."

"What exactly is forgiveness, anyway? I've always heard people say, 'Forgive and forget.' I'm not sure I *can* forget."

The older man nodded in agreement. "Actually, you're right. None of us can really forget the things that happen to us. A psychiatrist friend of mine tells me that everything that happens to us has been indelibly recorded in biochemical pathways in our brains."

"So if we can't forget, how do we forgive?" the young man insisted.

"Forgiveness is actually a choice. Let me tell you a story about Abraham Lincoln. It seems there was this guy who had made it his mission in life to discredit Lincoln. He did everything he could to drag Lincoln's reputation through the mud. He told stories that weren't true. Stirred up adversaries.

"But when Lincoln was elected president, he included this man on a list of appointees to public office. His advisors told Lincoln, 'You can't possibly consider appointing this guy. Don't you remember all those things he said about you during the campaign? All the things he did to try to discredit you?' As I heard the story, Lincoln looked his advisors in the eye, and said, 'I distinctly remembered forgetting those things.'"

As the older man paused for effect, his young protégé nodded, then hesitated. "I still don't think I could practice that kind of forgiveness."

"Actually any of us can practice that kind of forgiveness—with the right kind of motivation," the older man replied. Thumbing through his Bible, he pulled a 3x5 card from between two pages, looked at the words typed on it, then handed it to his friend. "This is from the same place where the apostle Paul wrote, 'If you are angry, don't sin by nursing your grudge.' It's also in the same place where he tells us to put away all bitterness, anger, harsh words, and ill will. The verse on this card explains what I mean by motivation to forgive."

The young man looked at the words on the card before him. "Be kind to each other, tenderhearted, forgiving one another, just as God has forgiven you because you belong to Christ."

"And God doesn't grade sin on a curve the way we sometimes do."

As he looked pointedly at his young visitor, the older man's blue eyes seemed to grow in intensity. "Have you been forgiven?" he asked.

"I guess so—I'm not sure. What are you getting at?"

"Well, it's like this. The essence of what being a Christian is all about is being forgiven. See that plaque on the wall over there? Read it."

The young man turned in his seat. His lips formed the words. "Christians aren't perfect. Just forgiven."

"Do you remember when Jesus was dying on the cross? He actually offered forgiveness to the men who were crucifying Him."

"Yeah, I think I do remember that. Didn't He say something like, 'Father forgive them, they know not what they do'?"

"That's right. Now, why do you think He was able to forgive them?"

The young man thought for a moment. "I'm not sure. It's hard to figure out. I mean, they deserved to die for what they did. But He sure didn't."

"That's the whole point. He actually died in their place. That's why God could forgive them. In fact, to forgive their sins actually means that God sends their sins away. You studied business administration, didn't you?"

"Sure." The young man smiled. "Got my MBA from one of the top schools in the country."

"So you must have studied accounting?"

"Yep."

"Then I think you'll be able to understand what forgiveness is all about. You see, our sins are on the debit side of the ledger. Everything we've ever done that was wrong. Every impure thought. Every careless word. Every bad deed.

"Only they're not on a ledger of wrongs committed against other people. They may have hurt other people, but they ultimately show up on the ledger of wrongs committed against God. That's what the Bible refers to when it talks about sin, when it describes us as sinners."

The young man thought for a moment about what he had been hearing. "I guess I always assumed that sins were major kinds of things: like murder or adultery. Actually I guess I felt like my wife was a pretty big hypocrite. After all, she seemed to be such a good Christian, and she committed adultery. I guess I haven't thought much about the fact that I fooled around quite a bit before we were married—especially while I was in college, even in high school. So I guess I'm just as bad a sinner as she is—or even that jerk from the museum."

The older man sat back in his chair. Holding his Bible up vertically for emphasis, he said, "God loves sinners, but He doesn't like sin. In fact, He hates sin. And God doesn't grade sin on a curve the way we sometimes do. He talks about lust in our hearts in the same breath with adultery, about hating a person in the same sentence as murder. One of the Proverbs lists seven things God hates. The first one is pride, the second lying. So I guess it's safe to say that sin is sin.

"And the penalty for sin, according to the Bible, is real simple. It's death. So when Jesus died, He wasn't just a martyr for a cause or a good example of some noble sacrifice. He was actually paying for the sins of the men who crucified Him. Plus, He was paying for your sins and mine. The Bible describes Him as the Lamb of God who takes away the sins of the world. So, if we've been forgiven, we can forgive others, because we will never face a situation where we have to forgive someone more than God has forgiven us."

"I think I get your point about bitterness. But doesn't God expect me to do certain things to be a Christian? I've sure been trying. Well, I guess sometimes I've been trying harder than at other times. But I've always thought God expected us to perform up to a certain level or we wouldn't be good enough for him."

"I suspect you're reading your dad back into your concept of what God is like," the older man responded. "Most of us tend to do that, especially if our dads have been harsh or critical. People who have dads who are extremely permissive and don't care what they do tend to feel like they're entitled to have the good things in life handed to them on a silver platter. They figure God won't hold them accountable.

All of us seem to get a warped idea of what God is like based on how we've been raised.

"But God isn't like any of our human parents. Not really. Even though He absolutely hates sin—hated it enough to allow Jesus, His only son, to die for it—He still loves us. He's like the father of the prodigal son in the Bible—always waiting for us to come back to Him. He never stops caring about us. He'll always accept us, and He wants to be close to us. He cares about what's going on in our lives."

"Aren't you preaching at me a little bit?" the young man responded tersely.

Glancing at his watch, the older man replied, "Maybe I am at that. Tell you what, we're past our time for today. Why don't you make a list for the next time we get together—a list of all the things you think a person has to do to be a Christian. Then we'll go over that list and talk about it together. Before you go, though, I want you to see one more thing."

Reaching into another folder in his file cabinet, the old man pulled out a piece of paper. "A number of years ago, a good friend gave me this. I still look at it regularly. Sort of as a reminder"

What the young man saw was a very simple message, part of which was printed in handwriting neater than the older man's, part of which was typeset:

EACH NEW DAY BRINGS THE CHOICE . . .
BITTER
OR
BETTER

"I think I'm beginning to see what you're getting at about bitterness," the young man said as got up to shake hands with his mentor.

3

AUTHENTIC FAITH

I made my list," announced the young man as he stepped into his mentor's office the following week. He handed the older man a folded sheet of paper.

The One Minute Christian quickly scanned the items on the list.

A Christian is one who

- attends church regularly
- does what is right
- reads his Bible
- gives to God
- keeps the Ten Commandments
- practices the Golden Rule
- forgives others who wrong him

"You know, I spent a lot of time thinking about this assignment," the young man said. "I hadn't really thought much about the subject since I was a kid. In fact, for a long time, I didn't think much about being a Christian. I just assumed I was one. After all, I even picked up a couple of church attendance pins when I was a kid.

"I was wrapped up in getting married, starting my career, trying to become a success in my job. Then I found out things were not so good in my marriage—or in my job. I guess it started me thinking more about the spiritual side of my life."

"That's fairly common," the older man replied. "I've talked to a lot of people recently who've been working hard at their careers, only to decide that there's more to life than driving the right car or being known as a successful company man."

The young man looked across the room at his colleague, a puzzled expression on his face. "There's something I couldn't quite figure. The last time we met you talked about forgiveness and forgiving others because we've been forgiven. That made a lot of sense. But I've never really thought much about that. I mean, sure I've done things that are wrong. When I do, I almost always ask God to forgive me. And usually, if I do something wrong—I mean really wrong—I try to make up for it, you know, by doing things right or looking for ways to help other people."

Leaning back in his chair, the older man nodded. "I think I see where you're coming from. Actually, your list tipped me off. Let's look at it together, OK? Why don't I write it on the board?"

Moving to the acrylic board, he picked up a marker and began reproducing the list he held in his hand.

"Let's see. A Christian

- ✔ goes to church
- ✔ forgives others
- ✔ does what's right
- ✔ reads the Bible
- ✔ gives to God
- ✔ keeps the Ten Commandments
- ✔ practices the Golden Rule"

When he had copied the list on the board, the older man turned to his young companion. "Have you noticed what all these things have in common?"

The young man scratched his chin and thought for a moment. "Well, for one thing, they're all religious activities—at least most of them are. Maybe some of the Ten

Commandments wouldn't be considered religious. But I guess if it's one of the top ten, it must be religious. Right?"

"I suppose so. But there's something else these all have in common. Think about it for a moment."

This time the young man paused for almost a minute. Finally, he broke the silence. "I don't see it. I guess you'll have to tell me what you're thinking."

"Think with me," the older man said. "Look at the verbs."

"Oh, yeah. High school English. Go, forgive, do, keep, have . . ."

"Right. But I'm not really trying to get off into grammar. What I want you to see is that all these verbs have something in common."

"You mean they're all something you *do*?" the young man asked.

"Exactly. Now let me see if I can point out a very important distinction. If someone were to ask you, 'How do I become a Christian?' would you tell him to do these things?"

The young man thought for a moment. "I guess so. I'd probably also tell him to believe in God. Isn't faith part of all this?"

"Ah!" said the older man. "Faith and works. What do they have to do with becoming a Christian?"

"I think they're both important. I mean, it's one thing to believe in God, but what's the point if your life isn't different? I mean, some of the guys I work with, they're absolute sharks—cutthroats." The young man's voice intensified. "They don't mind walking on other people to try to get to the top. They'll cheat, steal—even sell their own mothers! And some of them claim to be good Christians!"

"Good point. Maybe we'd better back up a step and raise another question. Ever heard the phrase, 'All roads lead to heaven'?"

"Sure," the young man responded, "but I don't believe it."

"Why do you think someone coined that phrase?"

"Probably because people teach so many different ways to become a Christian: join a certain church, be baptized, keep the Ten Commandments."

The older man paused for a moment, then continued. "And what do most of those ways have in common? Look at your list for a clue."

"I guess they all involve doing something."

"Right. Now here's the rub. Can you *do* something to become a Christian? You see, in our society, you can do something to become a husband—get married. You can do something to earn an MBA—pursue your degree and complete your course work. You can do something to become employed by a Fortune 500 company. But I don't have to tell you this—you've worked pretty hard at all of them. Have you worked at anything else?"

"Well, I play softball for a community team. I work pretty hard at that. I collect baseball trading cards—and I've started working pretty hard at these Christian things lately."

"A lot of people . . . hold the view that at the end of life God weighs their good deeds and their bad deeds."

"So you think that if a person does certain things, or does enough of them, he'll become a Christian?"

"I guess so. I really hadn't thought about it that much until now."

"How were you introduced to Christianity?" the older man asked.

"I was probably twelve or thirteen years old. They had some kind of special deal in our church for all the kids—we called it 'confirmation.' My parents told me it was how I became part of the Christian community. I remember that the minister used the words 'community of faith.' I just assumed that was some kind of an initiation rite, the way people became a Christian."

"Now that's interesting," the older man said. "Were you doing all the things on your list?"

"No."

"You considered that you were a Christian from that point?"

"Yeah, I guess so."

"What exactly did you do to become a Christian?"

"I don't really know. I attended church regularly. I remember the pastor talked about social justice, civil rights—when I was in college, I actually marched in a couple of demonstrations. So I sort of felt like I had enough concern and was sort of a Christian." The young man's face crinkled in puzzlement. "I guess I'm really confused now."

The older man responded with a smile. "You know, I've talked with a lot of people who were puzzled over this very thing. In fact, there's probably nothing more important to be clear about in your thinking. After all, it happens to be the one question that determines where we spend eternity."

Calling the young man by his first name, he continued. "A lot of people I've talked to hold the view that at the end of life God weighs their good deeds and their bad deeds. Is that sort of the way you've been seeing it?"

"Probably so. I've always figured there'd be a day of reckoning. The good would either outweigh the bad, or the other way around."

Walking over to his desk, the older man picked up his now familiar copy of Scripture and returned to the conference table. "Let me list some people from the Bible. You tell me if you think their good works outweighed their bad. Would God give them a thumbs up or a thumbs down?

"The apostle Paul."

"Oh, thumbs up, no question."

"Judas."

"Thumbs down."

"David."

"Probably thumbs up."

"Jezebel."

"Wasn't she that queen who had so many people killed? Thumbs down."

"Abraham."

"Thumbs up."

"So you think Abraham was right with God?"

"Sure, from what I remember about him in Sunday school. Wasn't he called a friend of God or something like that?"

Turning in his Bible to the fourth chapter of the book of Romans, the older man said, "Let's see if we can figure out what Abraham did to be right with God. Here, read these verses."

The young man began to read.

Abraham was, humanly speaking, the founder of our Jewish nation. What were his experiences concerning this question of being saved by faith? Was it because of his good deeds that God accepted him? If so, then he would have something to boast about. But from God's point of view Abraham had no basis at all for pride. For the Scriptures tell us Abraham *believed God*, and that is why God cancelled his sins and declared him "not guilty."

"Stop right there," the older man said. "That verse you just read, what does it mean?"

The young man examined the verse again, then looked up at his teacher. "I guess it's saying that works didn't make Abraham right with God."

"Exactly. In fact, he'd have really had something to brag about if he could have done something to make himself right with God. But he didn't. What *did* he do? Read it again."

The young man read where his companion was pointing. "'Abraham *believed God*, and that is why God cancelled his sins.' Oh, so you're saying, it's not works—it's faith."

"Am *I* saying that?" the older man asked. "Or is that what you're reading from the Bible. You see, my opinion doesn't count. What really matters is what God says. Look at the next two verses."

The young man resumed reading:

> But didn't he earn his right to heaven by all the good things he did? No, for being saved is a gift; if a person could earn it by being good, then it wouldn't be free—but it is! It is *given* to those who do *not* work for it. For God declares sinners to be good in his sight if they have faith in Christ to save them from God's wrath. King David spoke of this . . .

The older man interrupted him. "Let's stop right there. Earlier I mentioned three people from Scripture: Paul, Abraham, and David. Now, Paul wrote these words, Abraham is the subject, and now David's mentioned. Let's see if we can put this all together."

The young man thought, *He's getting too theoretical. He's losing me, and now I'll bet he's about to start preaching again.* But aloud he asked, "Are you telling me that none of these men were made right with God because of their good works? I'm not sure I can buy that."

"All three of these men were pretty good. But none of them was perfect. Abraham allowed another man to take his wife, just to save his own neck. David did the opposite: he took somebody else's wife—*after* he had him murdered! The woman's name was Bathsheba. And Paul—well, Paul actually had Christians arrested, even put to death."

"Wait a minute, now," the young man said, a hint of sarcasm creeping into his voice. "These people, they're somewhere back in the Bible. They don't live today. I mean, come on, we're at the end of the twentieth century."

"I get your drift. Maybe it worked that way back then, but not now?"

"Maybe."

The older man paused reflectively. "Ever hear of Chuck Colson?"

"Sure. Wasn't he one of the guys who went to prison after Watergate?"

"Yep. He had been one of the president's inner circle. By his own admission he was one of the up-and-coming young men in the Nixon White House. Said he gave up a better paying job because he really wanted to be able to be near the president—to have that kind of power and influence. But he ended up abusing that power."

"Right. But what does being a criminal have to do with being a Christian?"

"Well, just about the time Chuck Colson was sentenced to prison, somebody took the time to explain to him what it meant to be a Christian. Like a lot of people, he'd always assumed that he *was* a Christian. After all, he loved God, motherhood, and apple pie, though not necessarily in that order."

The young man smiled. "So how *did* he become a Christian?"

"The same way those ancient criminals did that I was talking about—David and Paul. He stopped trying to earn his way to heaven, stopped trying to be right with God on the basis of his good works. He admitted he had done wrong and trusted Christ to make his wrongs right."

"But that didn't keep him out of prison, did it?"

"No," his mentor replied. "You can be forgiven for sins but still have to suffer their consequences. It's sort of like a man who destroys his family and his liver by drinking. He may come to Christ and be freed from his addiction. But he can still wind up estranged from his family and in the hospital because of a ruined liver.

"Maybe a question will clarify what I'm getting at. How many crimes does it take to make a person a criminal? How many murders to make a person a murderer?"

The young man thought for a second. "Just one, I suppose."

"Exactly. Now, suppose you committed just one murder in your entire life. You went before the judge, looked him in the eye, and said, 'Judge, I have twenty character witnesses who will tell you that I've been a good, loving,

AUTHENTIC FAITH

upstanding citizen, husband, father, and employee all my life. I've never committed a murder before this, and I can assure you that I'll never do it again.' Would your verdict be innocent or guilty?"

"That's easy," the young man grinned. "I'd be as guilty as sin."

"Right. And I'm glad you brought up the subject of sin, because sin is the whole issue here."

"What do you mean?"

"You answered how many murders it takes to make a man a murderer. Now, how many sins does it take to make a person a sinner?"

"Um, just one, I guess."

"That's right. Now, let me show you something interesting."

Turning in his Bible to a book near the end of the New Testament, he handed the book to the young man and said, "Read this verse—James 2:10."

"'And the person who keeps every law of God, but makes one little slip, is just as guilty as the person who has broken every law there is.'

Man, that sounds tough. Sounds like if I've ever committed one sin, there's no way I can make up for it. Kind of shoots my way of thinking about things."

The older man smiled. "I think we're getting somewhere today. But let me tell you about a couple of people from totally different backgrounds. Both of them have the same first name—John.

"The first one was a man named John Wesley. He was one of the founders of the Methodist Church. Wesley came to America as a missionary. His mother had been a godly woman, and he certainly had heard a great deal of Christian teaching. He's the kind of person who, if you looked at his life, you'd figure he *had* to be a Christian. Let me show you his schedule."

Walking over to the filing cabinet in the corner of his room, the gray-haired man rummaged through a drawer,

63

pulled out a folder, removed a piece of paper, and brought it back to the conference table. "Read this."

The young man scanned the page, then began reading.

4:00 A.M.	– 5:00 A.M.	— Private Prayer
5:00 A.M.	– 7:00 A.M.	— Bible Reading
8:00 A.M.	– 9:00 A.M.	— Public Prayer
9:00 A.M.	– 12:00 noon	— Bible Study
12:00 noon	– 1:00 P.M.	— Testimony
2:00 P.M.	– 4:00 P.M.	— Witnessing

Pausing, the young man looked at his mentor. "Took an hour off for lunch, didn't he?"

4:00 P.M.	– 5:00 P.M.	— Evening Prayers
5:00 P.M.	– 6:00 P.M.	— Private Prayer
6:00 P.M.	– 7:00 P.M.	— Public Reading
7:00 P.M.	– 8:00 P.M.	— Evening Service
8:00 P.M.	– 9:00 P.M.	— Witnessing

The older man said, "As I calculate it, that's about four hours in prayer, five hours in witnessing, and six hours in Bible study. *Every day.* Would you think Wesley to be a Christian?"

"No doubt about it."

"Right! It all comes down to one thing. Trusting Jesus Christ to provide forgiveness for our sins through His death on the cross."

"Well, before I tell you the rest of John Wesley's story, let me tell you about this other guy. His name was John Newton. Like John Wesley, his mother taught him a great deal about the Christian faith. But Newton was interested in other things. By the time he reached his teens, he was a sailor. A rowdy young man, he joined the British Navy in

1745. But he went AWOL to see his girlfriend near Plymouth, England. He was arrested, flogged, and sold as a slave at the age of twenty. Eventually Newton went to a work for a man named Clough. For more than four years, he captained slave ships for him."

"Can't get much lower than that, can you?" the young man observed.

"No, but here's what's remarkable. Both Wesley and Newton came to the same conclusion. They weren't good enough to get to heaven by themselves. They had sinned and deserved whatever punishment a righteous God decided to give them.

"But here's what's really remarkable. Both men discovered from reading the Bible that Jesus Christ, God's son, had been punished in their place. That His death on the cross took the penalty they deserved. They discovered God's grace, the loving favor He extends to all of us.

"As a result, both men—one a religious man, a missionary, the other the captain of a slave ship, a trader in human lives—became Christians."

The older man looked directly at his friend and said, "Do you understand what I'm getting at?"

The young man thought before he replied. "I guess it doesn't matter how good or how bad we are."

"Right! It all comes down to one thing. Trusting Jesus Christ to provide forgiveness for our sins through His death on the cross."

Again calling the young man by his first name, he asked, "If you were to stand before God right this minute, or in the next five minutes, and He were to ask, 'Why should I let you into heaven?' how would you reply?"

The young man sat silently for what seemed like an eternity. There was a catch in his voice when he finally said, "I guess till now I would have handed God that same list I gave you, that stuff about going to church, keeping the Ten Commandments, forgiving others. That wouldn't work though, would it?"

"No. It didn't work for John Wesley. And of course, John Newton wouldn't have had much of a list at all. They were like Abraham, like Paul. They believed."

"But what does it mean to believe?" the young man asked.

"Well, that's pretty simple. You're sitting on a chair right now, aren't you?"

Glancing down, the young man said, "Sure. What's that got to do with it?"

"How did you come to be sitting in that chair?"

"When I came in, you invited me to have a seat."

"And you trusted me—and the chair, right?"

"Hm. I see."

The older man paused before he continued. "You see, all kinds of people have expressed their opinion about how to get to heaven. God, in the Bible, invites us to do only one thing: To trust His Son who died on the cross as our only way back to Him; to stop trying to earn salvation and come to the place where we trust Him with our life, our soul—like what you did with your body when you sat in that chair. Have you ever actually done that?"

The silence in the room was deafening as the young man scanned the floor. "I guess I haven't. I think when I was a kid I was just doing what people expected when I went forward in that church service. I didn't really understand. I attended those Bible studies when I was in college. I've done all those things at church recently. But I guess you're telling me I'm not a real Christian."

The older man smiled. "I'm just trying to tell you how God says we go about becoming a real Christian. You see, you've probably believed the facts about Christ. You know that He was God's son, that He was perfect, that He died on the cross, and that He rose again on the third day."

"Yeah, I've believed those for a long time."

"And you've probably even wanted to be right with God. In fact, I suspect that's what prompted your quest to find out about the One Minute Christian."

"Right again," the young man said. "So what's missing?"

"Well, the total you is composed of a mind that thinks, emotions that feel—and a will that chooses. Maybe it's time for you to exercise your will to place your trust in Jesus Christ personally."

"So how do I do that?"

"Well, it's not necessary to 'do' any particular thing. But a lot of the people I've talked to have come to the point you have, and they've simply told God in a prayer that they were putting their trust in His Son. It's sort of like a wedding. How do you become married?"

"You say, 'I do,'" the young man said.

The older man nodded. "And that's what this prayer would be. In effect, you'd be saying 'I do' to Jesus Christ—I do trust You to take away my sins, to give me new life. Would you like to do that?"

The silence lengthened as the young man thought about what he had been told. Glancing at his watch he said, "I guess I need to think about this. Is that a problem?"

"I don't think so. As long as you don't think about it for too long. It's not something to put off. God's offer is for real, just like God Himself. But He'll be there whenever you get ready to tell Him that you trust in Him. I'm looking forward to hearing that you did."

"I think I'm pretty close to ready," the young man replied. "But not today. No, not today. But I will think about it—seriously."

As he rose to leave, the older man thrust a book into his hand. "Here's a modern translation of the New Testament. Maybe it'll come in handy."

4

A BIG STEP

It was almost dark. The man known as the One Minute Christian was sitting in a corner booth at a coffee shop two blocks from his office, a half-cup of coffee in front of him. After he finished scanning the sports page of the paper he hadn't had time to read that morning, he glanced at his watch, then looked up at the door. The young man he had been waiting for came rushing in, almost colliding with a waitress who was carrying a full tray of food.

Offering his apologies, he looked around, quickly spotted his friend, and headed toward his table. His face was covered with a big smile.

"Thanks for meeting me," he said. "I felt like I needed to let you know that I think it's coming together. The other night I stayed up till nearly 3:00 A.M. My wife and I had another big argument—we're still having trouble getting things back together. Even with the counseling I'm not sure whose fault it is.

"Anyway, I took that New Testament you gave me and found the place where it talked about Abraham and David— you know, Romans 4."

The older man nodded, and his companion continued. "I kept thinking about this business of working to become a Christian, to please God. And I think you're right about that, on both counts."

The older man's face took on a puzzled look. "Both counts?" he asked. "What do you mean?"

"Well, for one thing, you told me God didn't operate on a performance basis. He loves us even if we've blown it. What do you call that? Grace?"

"Right. But what's the other count?"

"Well, I've thought about it for a long time, and it really made me mad when you first suggested it. But I think you have a point. I guess part of my problem is that I've always thought of God as being sort of like my dad—somebody who was there to punish me when I did wrong but otherwise wasn't too involved in my life. I think I'm getting a different perspective about God now. I'm not sure I'm a whole lot farther down the road than I was, but I'm beginning to see things differently.

"You know, when I was in college, I sort of followed the party line of the profs I studied under. I thought it was cool to be an agnostic, to deny the existence of God—or to say you really couldn't know for sure that He existed.

"I'm a good deal older than I was back in those days. And the more I've thought about it, the more I think God really does exist. You seem pretty sure about God. In fact, from what I've seen of you, it's like you talk to him every day. But how do you know you're not being fooled?"

"I think there are probably three main reasons I don't have any doubt about whether God exists or what He's like. And there's one of the reasons."

With his eyes the young man followed the older man's extended finger. Through the window of the restaurant he saw the rays of the setting sun, a panoply of colors from bright orange and gold to brilliant red and deep purple, filling the western sky.

"Just look at that sunset!" the gray-haired man exclaimed. "And it's only one small part of creation. It's impossible for me to think that such a complex universe came about by chance. And that's the evolutionist's formula: 'the impersonal plus time plus chance.' In fact, that's the only option, unless you accept a creator."

Pointing to his wristwatch, the older man continued. "I've noticed you wear one of these also." The young man looked somewhat embarrassed as he pulled back his mono-grammed sleeve to expose the expensive Rolex on his left wrist.

"There's quite a difference in the cost of these two watches, but both have two things in common."

"I guess one is pretty obvious. They both tell time. What's the other one?"

"Tell you after this thirty-second time-out," the older man said as the waitress came to refill his coffee cup and hand the young man a menu.

He asked her to fill his cup with coffee too. After the waitress moved on, the older man picked up where he left off. "The other thing these two watches have in common? Neither one of them happened by chance. One is a lot more expensive than the other, but both give evidence of an intelligent designer."

Stirring his coffee thoughtfully, the young man replied, "That's what those guys in my fraternity used to tell me. I got into a lot of arguments with them over creation and evolution. They kept telling me the universe was too complex to have just happened."

"From what you've been telling me,
God's supposed to be really good.
If he's that good, and if things are
as bad as they are, what's the deal?"

The older man paused to add sweetener to his coffee, stirred it, took a sip, then set his cup down carefully. "You've studied computers haven't you?" he asked his companion.

"Pretty extensively."

"Do you remember when *Time* magazine voted the computer the machine of the year?"

"That's been quite a few years ago now, hasn't it?"

"1983, I believe," said the older man. "Here's my point. Even with all the complexities of computers—and today they can do a lot more than they did in 1983—they haven't come close to the intelligence of the human brain. I was reading about it the other day. Three pounds of jelly-like mass made up of between ten and a hundred billion neurons. Each neuron as complex as a small computer, all by itself. According to this book I was reading, each brain cell sends messages through synapses to other brain cells by means of electrical impulses. It's all so complex—the brain can't even begin to comprehend its own complexity. Another writer I read suggested that the number of connections within one human brain may be as great as the total number of stars in all the galaxies in the universe. I just can't conceive of something like that happening by chance."

The young man held up his hand impatiently. "OK, OK. So there probably is a God. But I still have trouble figuring out why there's so much evil in the world. I mean it seems like there's some new atrocity every day! People shooting innocent bystanders, murdering young children. Terrorists blowing up airplanes. What about the innocent people on Pan Am flight 103? Those people didn't deserve to die! I mean, imagine you're flying home from the holidays. One minute you're eating a meal on a plane, the next you're blown into oblivion."

"Those things bother me too. I guess that's been one of the classic questions about God."

Quickly the young man responded, "I mean, from what you've been telling me, God's supposed to be really good. If he's that good, and if things are as bad as they are, what's the deal? Look at this guy Jeffrey Dahmer, up in Milwaukee. He did horrible things to people—I mean, it makes me sick just to read about them. Then there was that guy Bundy, down in Florida. How many girls did he murder? And the guy who died not too long ago—Richard Speck? He's the one who killed all those nurses in Chicago—that's been years ago. How can a good God let people like that kill one innocent person after another?"

"I'm not sure I can fully answer that question," the older man said gently. "But I think the key to it is understanding that God didn't just make people to be robots. He gave each of us a free will, a right to choose. The problem is, we humans started choosing to go against His will as far back as Adam and Eve."

"Our first parents," the young man replied sarcastically. "So they're to blame."

"Yes and no," the One Minute Christian replied calmly. "They're to blame in the sense that they really started the whole business of choosing to go against God. But there's also a sense in which each of us is responsible for our own choices."

"I guess it's like you said the other day. Everybody's a sinner, right?"

"That's how the Bible explains it. Remember the article in the paper the other day? About babies born with the HIV virus?"

A look of anger crossed the young man's face. "Boy, do I? Talk about something *really* unfair."

"I agree. But that's the whole point. Every single one of the babies in the nurseries of every hospital in this country has been infected by the sin virus—because there hasn't been a baby born yet who had perfect parents."

"Wasn't Jesus the exception to that rule?"

"No. Actually, He wasn't. According to the Bible, He was perfect, but neither His mother Mary nor His stepfather Joseph was perfect. In fact, Mary even admitted in a prayer that God had been merciful toward her in her lowly state and that she needed a Savior.

"But there's another side to the whole issue. That's choice. Not only is everybody born with a nature polluted by sin, we all grow up *choosing* to be sinners. Do you have younger brothers and sisters?"

"Sure. I didn't get along too well with them though."

"Do you suppose part of that has to do with the fact that they were sinners?"

The young man grinned. "No question about that."

"Let's get back to what we were talking about. You were asking me how I know God exists. One reason is creation. The other one is the Bible."

"That raises another question for me. I know the Bible talks about God, but it seems like circular reasoning. How can you prove God from the Bible and prove the Bible from God all at the same time?"

Undeterred, the older man shifted his position in the booth, took a sip from his water, then responded. "I guess you could look at it that way, except that wouldn't take into account the uniqueness of the Bible. You see, the Bible is different from any other book ever written. More than forty authors contributed to its writing over a fifteen-hundred year period of time. They came from every walk of life. Paul was a rabbi, Moses was trained in politics. Peter was a fisherman, with no formal education. Matthew was a tax collector —sort of like an IRS agent. And Amos, one of the prophets, was a farmer. In fact, he referred to himself as a 'fig picker.' That in itself is unique enough. What's really amazing is that, even though the Bible addresses hundreds of controversial topics, these authors never contradicted each other."

The young man interrupted. "But what about all the mistakes in the Bible? Don't we have a lot of missing pieces as far as the original text goes?"

"Actually, there's more evidence for the original text of the Bible than for the original manuscripts of the plays of Shakespeare. And Shakespeare was writing in the seventeenth century—after printing was invented.

"Besides all that, hundreds of prophecies given during biblical times have been fulfilled precisely. Suppose you'd been living in about 1875 and someone asked you to predict the name of the man who would be president of the United States in 1988. How would you respond?"

"I'd laugh," the young man replied. "All those predictions Jeanne Dixon and people like that make—I think they're ridiculous."

"They are for the most part, because they never come true. But there's a remarkable prediction in the Bible. About seven hundred years before Christ, a man named Isaiah actually named the world ruler who would give the command to rebuild Jerusalem's Temple. At the time he wrote, Babylonia was the most powerful nation in the world. And it was pretty evident that it would soon conquer Israel.

"There are some things that can't be understood completely. We just have to take them by faith."

"But nobody had a clue that a man named Cyrus would come along who would conquer Babylon—except those people who read what Isaiah wrote. So about 535 B.C. —about 160 years after Isaiah wrote his prophecy—a Persian king named Cyrus did exactly what Isaiah predicted. He issued a decree giving permission to rebuild the Temple in Jerusalem. That's just one of hundreds of prophecies fulfilled in the Bible. If you're interested, there's a book I picked up several years ago that talks about these kinds of questions in detail. It's called *Evidence That Demands a Verdict.* It was written by a man I've come to respect highly since I've gotten to know him personally. His name is Josh McDowell."

"Wait a minute," the young man interrupted. "Josh McDowell? Doesn't he debate people on college campuses?"

"He has."

"I remember hearing him once when I was in college. He debated one of our philosophy profs. I didn't like a lot of what he had to say at the time. But I remember he stood his ground pretty well. He seemed to have an answer for everything the prof threw at him."

"I'll get you a copy of his book," the older man responded, making a note in his Day Timer, which lay open on the table in front of him. "I think it will answer a lot of the questions you have about God and the Bible. But I want you to remember something—you'll *never* get all the answers to every one of your questions. There are some things that can't be understood completely. We just have to take them by faith.

"Take those lights coming on out there," the older man pointed to the window, where street lamps and other lights were coming to life against the nearly-dark evening sky. "Do you understand how electricity works? I don't. I mean, I've read about positive and negative charges, and all that. But I don't fully understand it. I have a friend who's an electrical engineer. He admits he doesn't understand it all, either. Says he's not sure even Edison had all the answers. But he says we have to try to understand what we can—and take the rest by faith."

"What do you mean?" the young man queried. "We need to use our minds. We can't just check them at the door, can we—I mean, about religious things? After all, we try to come up with reasonable answers about everything else!"

"Sure. But I don't think faith and reason are incompatible. Take the field of medicine for example. Ever had surgery?"

"Once," the young man replied. "Had my appendix out a few years ago."

"OK. How much did you understand about surgical procedures when you went under the knife?"

"Quite a bit, actually," the young man said, with a smug look. "I read everything I could get my hands on. Talked to several surgeons I knew—even went up to the hospital and observed an operation a couple of days before I had mine!"

"You were pretty thorough about it. So I guess your appendectomy wasn't one of those acute rush jobs."

"No, it wasn't. And that gave me time to check things out pretty carefully."

The older man shifted positions in his chair. "But you still had to trust that surgeon. I mean, you didn't actually stay awake to watch him operate on you."

The young man nodded in response. Scratching his chin, he replied, "I think I see what you're getting at. It's OK to check things out—but there's only so much checking we can do. At some point we have to just take it by faith. Is that what you mean?"

"Right. I hope you'll keep thinking about trust. Trusting surgeons. Trusting lights to come on when we flip the switch. Trusting airplanes when we fly—and pilots and air traffic controllers."

"Now there's something that *really* takes a lot of faith," the young man retorted as he reached for the check. "Especially tomorrow. I fly to Chicago—into O'Hare. Now that's scary. That takes a lot of faith!"

5

THE BIGGEST STEP

The gray-haired man circled the airport pick-up ramp again. Glancing at his watch, he scanned the crowd of deplaning passengers for his friend. The 2:35 P.M. flight from Chicago should have been at the gate by now. He had called the airline just before he left his office and was told that the flight was within five minutes of being on time. He was pretty sure his friend hadn't checked any luggage. He seemed like the kind of person who traveled light—probably just an overnight bag.

Pulling in just behind a cab, the older man thought about his young friend. At times he really seemed close to faith, to understanding what this business of trust was all about. But then those persistent questions seemed to get in the way—about values in life, money, even the evil in the world.

Suddenly he spotted the familiar face of the young man—neatly dressed in a gray double-breasted suit, carrying a slim, leather briefcase, a camel-hair overcoat, and a leather suit bag. Flashing his lights, he attracted the young man's attention.

"Thanks for picking me up," the young man said as he shook hands with his mentor. "Here—I'll just set these things in the back seat if that's OK. Hardly even needed this coat—thought it might be cool in Chicago, but it was pretty warm the whole week."

"So how do you like Chicago?" the older man asked as the two men fastened their seat belts.

"I've enjoyed the times I've been there. I stayed at a place just north of the Loop—rode the train back out to O'Hare this morning. Had a chance to circle the entire Loop before changing to the Douglas-O'Hare line.

"But being in downtown Chicago, seeing homeless people on the streets, riding the train through several really poor neighborhoods to O'Hare—I mean, it made me wonder again about some of those same questions we've been talking about the last few weeks."

The older man carefully maneuvered his car into the line of traffic headed for the airport exit and the expressway. "You said you left your car downtown at your office parking garage?"

"That's right. I rode to the airport with Charlie—he was flying to Denver. I really appreciate you picking me up. I could have grabbed a limo or a cab—but I wanted to talk to you anyway. Glad you had the time available."

"No problem—things were pretty flexible today." The older man accelerated into the expressway traffic. He slipped past a transit bus, then eased back into the right-hand lane. "You were saying about those questions?"

"Yeah. I mean, there are a lot of homeless people in parts of downtown Chicago. I saw them several times—one evening, the only night it was cool, we walked several blocks to a restaurant. Had some of the best pork chops I've ever eaten. Place called Morton's. But there were homeless people, street people. And a girl even propositioned one of the men with us, right there on the street. I mean, how can a good God let things get so bad?

"Then I got a call from a good friend of mine. He's one of the most conscientious, hard-working people I know. And one of the top people at what he does. But he's losing his job. His supervisor called him in, told him he wasn't performing up to standards, and gave him forty-five days to get his act together, or he was out of there. And he will be, too, I believe. His boss gave him a list of things to do that *three* people couldn't get done in six weeks! The guy has three little kids, and his wife's been sick. I mean, where is a good God in all this?"

Glancing sideways at his companion, the older man noticed the set of the young man's jaw, the glint in his eye. "I still don't have any easy answers. I guess it all comes down to the fact that all those things you mentioned—and what we talked about last week—are the fallout from sin. I mean, it's a plague, and all of us are affected to some degree. But those are things that makes God's favor that much more amazing. He cares about every one of us. Whether we choose to respond to Him or not."

"But what about those criminals we talked about? Jeffrey Dahmer, Ted Bundy, and Richard Speck—I thought about him while I was riding the train through those poor neighborhoods in Chicago. I mean, Speck just went into a boarding house and killed a bunch of nurses he didn't even know! And Bundy—what a monster! Killing people all over the country, hunting them down. How could God do anything but hate someone like that?"

The young man paused, sensing the intensity of his words. He slumped back into his seat apologetically. "I guess I'm just tired after being on the road this week. But it's hard to figure out. I didn't plan to bring this up again—I had something else to tell you."

"None of us is perfect. But perfect is how we'd have to be in order for God to accept us without Christ. And perfect is what none of us can ever be. . . . That's why we need to trust Christ."

"That's OK. I'm glad you felt free to let me in on how you feel about those things. Tell you what. Do you have time to grab a cup of coffee before I drop you off?"

"Sure," the young man replied. "I just need to pick some things up at the office before I head home—and my wife isn't expecting me until later. In fact, maybe the later the better."

Noticing his mentor's curious expression, he explained. "We had another argument on the phone last night. It wasn't very pretty."

Spotting a coffee shop at the next exit, the older man wheeled into the parking lot. The two men entered the restaurant, were seated, and ordered coffee. Then the older man picked up the thread of their conversation.

"You mentioned Ted Bundy. Did you know that he was forgiven before he died?"

"You've got to be kidding? God—forgave him?"

"That's what I heard. I caught part of an interview on the radio. I think it was recorded right before he was executed. Evidently he talked to this psychologist, Dr. James Dobson, who's a Christian. He said Bundy confessed what he had done and asked God to forgive him. Said he died at peace with God."

"But *we're* not that bad," the young man objected, his voice rising. "I mean, I'm not perfect, that's for sure. But—" His voice trailed off.

The older man sipped his coffee, then continued. "Maybe that's the point. None of us is perfect. But perfect is how we'd have to be in order for God to accept us without Christ. And perfect is what none of us can ever be. I mean, you did well in college and graduate school. But only a 4.0 grade point is perfection. And once you get a 'B' you've lost it forever. You have the ability to pick investments, but with your first bad stock choice you've lost your perfect track record for all time."

When the young man nodded, he continued.

"That's why we need to trust Christ. Nobody can work hard enough to make up for not being perfect."

The booth was silent as both men sipped their coffee. Then the young man smiled. "So we're back to trust, eh? But I have a question for you."

The young man paused, swallowed, and seemed to have difficulty continuing. Then he smiled again. "The other night, in Chicago, I sat up late. I kept reading those verses you pointed out to me about Abraham and David. I kept thinking about Abraham working to please God, and the difference when he stopped working and started trusting.

"Well, that's when it dawned on me—right there in the middle of the night, sitting at the desk in my hotel room. There really is a God out there. He does care about me, even though I haven't cared a lot about Him at times. And His son Jesus died in my place.

"So I started talking to Him, right there in my room. I told Him I trusted Him—that I didn't understand a lot about it, that I still had a lot of questions—but I wanted to trust Him.

"That's why I called you this morning to see if you could pick me up at the airport. I felt like you'd want to know—and I wasn't sure I could tell you over the phone."

The older man reached across the table to grip the hand of his young friend in a sort of modified high-five. "I'm really glad," was all he could say.

For a time the two men just sat there, savoring the moment. Then the older man leaned back in the booth and asked, "And how do you feel about what you did?"

"Pretty good. But I'm not sure I feel that different."

"That's not a problem. In fact, it's not a matter of feeling. Some people feel quite different. Others don't feel that different at all. The important thing is if you genuinely stopped trusting yourself or your works to be right with God and started trusting Jesus Christ."

"That's what I did."

"And that's why God says you've been forgiven—just like John Wesley, and just like John Newton. Newton is the man who wrote the hymn that was so popular it even became a best-selling pop tune—'Amazing Grace.'"

"I sort of vaguely remember that," the young man said. "I think Judy Collins recorded it. But I'm still not sure I really understand what grace is."

"The best explanation I ever heard is that grace is God giving us the opposite of what we deserve. In other words, because Jesus took the punishment we deserved to get, God gives us a new life—and everything that goes with it."

"Maybe that's why I feel like I'm starting all over again."

Outside, the traffic rushed past on the freeway. In the coffee shop, business seemed to be picking up. Reaching into his Day Timer, the older man extracted a 3x5 card. Taking his pen from his pocket, he began quickly printing a series of words. "I'm printing this so you can read it—there are only about three people in America who can read my handwriting—and I'm not one of them. And I'm doing it from memory. So it's probably worded differently from the way it is in your Bible."

He handed the card across the table. The young man looked at it and began to read:

> He who hears my words
> and believes Him who sent me
> has everlasting life
> and will never come into judgment,
> but has passed from death into life.
>
> (John 5:24)

"Keep this card handy. Whenever you have questions about what you did the other night in Chicago—and you probably will from time to time—pull it out. Look at it carefully. And remember, this is not my opinion. It's what Jesus Himself said in the Bible. There's a lot more to learn my friend, but you've taken a very big step—in fact, the biggest."

"Speaking of taking a big step—I have a big presentation at work tomorrow, and I've got to go back by the office. By the way, I think you must have been praying for me and my wife. We're actually beginning to talk a little bit. It's still tough at times—sometimes even explosive, like last night on the phone. But then we actually did talk, after the fireworks died down. I think the counseling is helping. We have another appointment tomorrow. And I guess what you told me about forgiveness is helping me put this into perspective."

"Talking to God and talking to your wife. Now that's really good. See you next week?"

"See you then." Pulling a money clip from his pocket, the young man quickly dropped a ten dollar bill on the table. "The coffee's on me, and so is the tip. No argument now. You've already given me a lot."

6

WHOLEHEARTED LOVE FOR GOD

We've been getting together for several weeks now," the young man began as he entered the office of the One Minute Christian. He was dressed in a gray, blended suit that John Malloy would have been proud of, a muted paisley tie, a blue, oxford button-down shirt, and genuine calfskin wing-tip shoes. "I really think it's time you told me what is the most important thing God wants me to do. Help me understand—what's top priority?"

Rising from his desk, where he had been rearranging a stack of notes, the older man walked around to shake hands with his young visitor. He was dressed in a light-blue patterned sport shirt and navy slacks. His hair, thinning on top, was a bit mussed, and his shoes needed polishing. "Are we in a bit of a hurry today?"

"Not at all—well, I guess you could say that. After all, I'm really a Christian now, at least since last week. Before that, I was trying to earn God's approval by what I did. But now I understand that being a Christian is a whole different ball game."

"Hey, speaking of ball games," the older man interjected, "how would you like to join me for a baseball game? There's a holiday next week, and one of my favorite teams is in town. The pitcher's not much younger than me, and I just happen to have tickets for two excellent seats. We'll have a chance to discuss some important things and have fun at the same time. And I sometimes enjoy doing two things at once, especially when one of them is having fun."

The young man's thoughts were impatient. *Why does this guy never seem to be in a hurry? He's exasperating! I mean, it's time to get on with things.* Aloud he asked, "Do you think we'll get anything done if we go to a ball game? I don't want to waste time. I need to find out what's important for me to do." The young man's voice trailed off.

His older colleague did not reply, and the silence grew until it filled the room. Finally, with a shy grin on his face, the young man shook his head and said, "Sorry. I guess I'm being a bit intense, aren't I? Here you are, taking time out of your schedule to meet with me. If anyone should be concerned about rushing things, I think it should be you. But you don't seem concerned at all."

The older Christian smiled and, with a sweep of his arm, gestured toward a wall where several degrees and certificates were displayed. "See if you can pick out the most important item on that wall," he challenged his friend.

The young man got up and began to carefully examine the items. They included a college degree, a certificate of appreciation for work in a summer program, membership in a national college careers society, a professional certificate, a graduate degree, and an appreciation plaque from a ministry organization.

"It must be either the graduate degree or this professional certificate—I'm not sure which. But it's probably not this little plaque here."

"Oh, my friend, but it is!" The older man grinned. "That's it! That's the most important item on that entire wall. Read it, and you'll see why."

The young man leaned over and scrutinized the calligraphic words:

God Is More Concerned
With Who I Am
Than With What I Do.

With an incredulous look on his face, the young man argued, "How can that be more important than a graduate degree or a professional certificate? I mean, I'm not even sure I agree with what it says!"

"Come, sit down," the older man instructed. He rose and moved toward the comfortable chairs grouped around the conference table in the other corner of the office. He opened the curtains to allow sunshine into the room, then seated himself.

The young man took another seat, a frown making a furrow in his forehead. But he resisted the temptation to continue arguing with his mentor. He simply waited to see what he would be told.

"Let me tell you why I consider that particular plaque to be more important than some of those so-called life achievement certificates and degrees."

Propping his feet on the corner of the table, the older man leaned back. He gazed out the window and ran his hand through his hair. "You see, there was a time when I was convinced God was far more concerned with what I did. In fact, at that point, I wasn't particularly concerned with who I was as long as I did those things I felt were pleasing to God. I was really into earning his approval."

Leaning forward, the young man interrupted. "Were you a Christian at that time, or were you like I was before last week?"

"Good question. Actually at that point, I had trusted Christ. But I was like some of the Christians Paul wrote to in the New Testament, in the book called Galatians. I had begun in the Spirit, trusting Christ as my Savior—but I was trying to continue my Christian life in the flesh—in a sort of 'performance trap.' I didn't understand the point of this verse."

Pulling a 3x5 card from his pocket, he placed it on the table in front of his young companion. Taking the hint, the young man picked up the card and recognized the printing style of his mentor.

"Read it," the older man encouraged.

"As you have therefore received Christ Jesus the Lord, so walk in Him. (Colossians 2:6)" (NKJV)

"I'm not sure I get it either," the young man said as he stared at the card, scratching his chin. "I guess you'll have to clue me in."

"You just received Christ Jesus last week. How did you receive Him?"

"By trusting Him. By faith."

"You didn't have to do anything or perform anything?"

"Not according to what you told me."

"And what was the basis for my telling you that?"

"Those verses you've been showing me in the Bible."

"Exactly," the older man said. Taking his feet off the desk, he leaned toward his younger colleague and pointed to the card on the table in front of him. "Paul says we are to walk in Him the same way we received Him. Do you get it now?"

"If you mean walk by faith, I think so."

"That's exactly what I mean. You see Paul and other New Testament writers used the word *walk* as a sort of summary word to describe the experience of living. So what Paul is saying is to live as a Christian the same way you became a Christian—by faith, by depending on God."

"I'm still not sure I understand all of what you're driving at."

"You're still married, aren't you?"

"So far. Remember I told you the other day, my wife and I are beginning to communicate better. I think we're learning how to forgive each other."

"Here's a question for you. Do you do things in order to stay married? For example, when you got married, did you promise to provide for your wife financially just in order to keep her from leaving you? Have you been keeping your marriage vows just to make sure she wouldn't bail out?"

The young man thought for a moment, looked out the window, then turned back to his mentor. "I don't think so.

In fact, I'm sure I don't. I do those things because I'm married. It just sort of goes with the territory."

"Precisely. You see, marriage is a relationship. It entails responsibilities, but it isn't primarily a responsibility. When you're enjoying a relationship, you're well beyond the stage where you keep certain rules. It's a difference in motivation. That was one of the toughest lessons for me to learn in life. And you know who taught me this lesson? A woman."

Remembering the cheerful lady who was the One Minute Christian's secretary, he asked, "It wasn't your secretary, was it?"

The older man chuckled. "Well, no and yes."

"Don't you mean yes and no?"

"No, she wasn't the primary person I learned the lesson from. But, yes, she helped teach me the lesson. You see, my secretary and several other people I've worked with used to be driven people, like me—and like you. All Type As. When we got started on a project, we'd often work right through mealtimes. One day we paused to snarf a few sandwiches for lunch—even though it was about 3:30 in the afternoon. I asked my secretary to bless the food, and she prayed, 'Lord, help us get everything done. Now, please. And in order. Amen.'"

"Didn't even mention the food, did she?" The two men laughed together. "Sounds like you guys were really a group of workaholics."

"No doubt about it," the older man replied. "But about that time I began studying the lives of two women in the New Testament. Their names were Martha and Mary. They were sisters, but they were as different as night and day."

Reaching across to pick up the Bible from the edge of his desk, the older Christian turned to the tenth chapter of Luke's gospel. "You see, Jesus and his disciples came to visit these two ladies often. Once, He was in one part of the house teaching, and Mary was sitting there, soaking up His words. Martha was in another part of the house, trying to get a meal ready. Luke observed that she was actually 'tied up in knots' about her serving.

"Finally Martha had had enough. She actually interrupted Jesus to say, 'Sir, doesn't it seem unfair to you that my sister just sits here while I do all the work? Tell her to come and help me.' Now, what do you think the Lord said at that point?"

"I'm still not sure I agree with your premise," the young man interrupted. "It just doesn't seem consistent with God not to be primarily concerned with what I do."

"He probably urged Mary to go help her sister."

"That's what I would have thought. In fact, if I had been Jesus, that's what I would have done. But that's not what He did at all. Read these next two verses—41 and 42."

"But the Lord said to her, 'Martha, dear friend, you are so upset over all these details! There is really only one thing worth being concerned about. Mary has discovered it—and I won't take it away from her.'"

Still looking down at the page, the young man gently shook his head. "Surprising," was the only word he said.

"Sure is, isn't it? See how it ties in with the plaque on my wall? Martha was living intensely—on a performance basis—just like you. And just like I used to live. She was so anxious—tied up in knots, really—about everything! She really felt it was important to always be doing something worthwhile.

"Mary, on the other hand, was more concerned with the relationship.

The older man paused, ran his hand through his graying hair, then resumed his train of thought. The young man listened intently.

"Now when I began sharing what I'd learned from Martha and Mary with the people around me—my colleagues at work and the people to whom I spoke in seminars, I began noticing distinctive changes—both in them, and in me."

"Including your secretary?"

"She caught on quickly. In fact, she told me it was like there was a Martha within, who was always eager to perform. She said that insight gave her a measure of freedom she had never experienced before."

"And your other colleagues?"

"Oh, they're much less driven now. Most of them have become almost as laid back as I have. But they're even more successful than they used to be. Several are in strategic management positions—and doing well, by the way."

"But there is another side of the coin," the older Christian continued. "Now that we've talked about how unconcerned God is with what you do, let me answer your original question about what we *are* to do."

"I'm still not sure I agree with your premise," the young man interrupted. "It just doesn't seem consistent with God not to be primarily concerned with what I do." *I'll bet he's going to tell me I got that from my dad.*

"It's natural to pick up our ideas of God from our human fathers."

I knew it!

"It's like wearing sunglasses." Taking a pair of clip-ons from his shirt pocket, the older man held them up to the light. "If I put these on, everything I look at, including you, is colored by them. I read somewhere that we are shaped to a great degree by what we learned between the ages of zero and six—perhaps 75-80 percent of our thinking and feelings—and especially our underlying beliefs. And of course our parents were the biggest influences in our lives."

"So I guess you're telling me that I'm still looking at God through the sunglasses of my father?"

"That's a pretty good way to put it."

He leaned across the table, turned a few well-worn pages in the copy of Scripture, then pointed to a paragraph in Mark's gospel. "This is Mark's account of a confrontation that occurred near the end of Jesus' ministry, just before He was crucified. There were several groups of people gathered around Jesus: Pharisees, Sadducees, Herodians—none of them liked each other, but all of them liked Jesus even less. They were asking Him all sorts of trick questions, trying to trip Him up. But He handled every question.

"One of the Scribes noticed how well Jesus answered their questions and raised an issue that, on the surface, seemed like just another trick question. That's it, at the end of verse 28."

Taking his cue, the young man read, "So he asked, 'Of all the commandments, which is the most important?'" Looking up, the young man asked, "Isn't that my question?"

"You could say that. This could have been just another a trick question—but the Scribes and Pharisees, who took the law seriously, frequently held debates over which commandments were more important than others."

"So they were like me. They wanted to know what was the most important commandment."

"But notice how Jesus answered him."

The young man looked down and resumed reading. "Jesus replied, 'The one that says "Hear, O Israel! The Lord our God is the one and only God. And you must love him with all your heart and soul and mind and strength."'"

As the young man looked up, his mentor said, "You know what really struck me about this? The first commandment is to *love.* That's the same lesson I learned from Mary and Martha. My primary responsibility is to the relationship. In fact, I call this commandment 'Wholehearted Love for God.' Do you see why?"

"I guess because He said to love the Lord with all your heart. That certainly sounds like 'wholehearted.'"

"What do you think of when you hear the word *heart?*"

The young man leaned back in his chair, stroked his chin, his brow furrowed in thought. "I guess coronary disease, heart failure, heart attacks—but that's not what Jesus had in mind."

"No. Jesus was using the term *heart* the same way most of the people in His day did. When they used the word *heart*, they generally referred to the immaterial part of man —the core of our being—the part of us with which we think, feel, and decide. That's what Solomon, the wisest king in history, meant when he said, 'Keep your heart with all diligence, for out of it spring the issues of life'" (NKJV).

The young man interrupted with a challenging tone in his voice. "But this is stuff from history. Centuries ago. I mean, we're living in days when people use their heads. I have a stack of books at home that I plan to read to sharpen my skills as a manager—books like *Leadership Secrets of Atilla the Hun, Tough-Minded Leadership*—"

Now it was the older man's turn to interrupt. *"Tough-Minded Leadership?* You mean by Joe Batten? You have a copy of that book?"

"Sure do. Are you familiar with it?"

"As a matter of fact, I met Joe last year. He was here for a business symposium with Hal Harris, who's a close friend of his. He actually gave me a copy of *Tough-Minded Leadership.*" Pulling a hard-cover book from his bookshelf, he opened it to a page that had been turned down and began reading.

> What some have characterized as flabby management is indeed widely practiced in this country. The answer to flabbiness, however, is not hardness or knee-jerk reactions using compressive force. Using rank as the first expedient has no place in the toolbox of the tough-minded leader.
>
> We must place a premium on developing the kind of sensing and intuitive skills that can only flow from the mind that is tough, resilient, open and questing, and from a heart that truly loves all customers and all members of the team.[1]

The young man looked over the shoulder of his mentor. He noticed he'd drawn a circle around the word *heart* and placed a star in the margin of this section.

1. Joe D. Batten, *Tough-Minded Leadership* (New York: AMACOM, 1989), p. 7.

The older man continued. "I had a chance to spend a few minutes interacting with Joe Batten about his tough-minded management and leadership concepts. I really thought we would be poles apart in our viewpoint, but I discovered Joe holds the same perspective I do. He's convinced that the heart and mind are the key issues. Solomon's father, David, is sort of a standard for whole-hearted love for God. Paul, in the New Testament, referred to him as a man after God's heart."

"Psychologists today generally divide the human personality . . . into intellect, emotions, and will. . . . Before psychology ever existed, Jesus identified these divisions and said that He wanted all of them focused on Him. That's what this business of wholehearted love for God is all about."

Before the older man could continue, his young companion asked, "Now what does a phrase like that mean? How can you be 'after somebody's heart'?"

"Well, it's not easy to explain. But I think the point is that David thought about things the way God did. He wanted to please God—tried to make decisions based on what he thought God wanted him to do. In other words, his relationship with God permeated every part of his life.

"In fact, David wrote in one of the Psalms, 'I have thought much about your words, and stored them in my heart that they would hold me back from sin' (119:11). Once he even prayed, 'Search me, O God, and know my heart; test my thoughts. Point out anything you find in me that makes you sad, and lead me along the path of everlasting life' (139:23)."

"Sounds like he thought his heart was pretty important," the young man observed.

"No doubt about it. Jesus once explained that the mouth speaks out of the abundance of the heart. But we have to remember that *heart* refers to more than just the emotions. That's why Jesus told that young scribe to love the Lord with all his heart—that was the summary statement. Then he added with all your soul (or emotions), with all your mind (your mental faculties), and with all your strength (what you choose with your will to do).

"Psychologists today generally divide the human personality the same way—into intellect, emotions, and will. I think it's intriguing that, before psychology ever existed, Jesus identified those divisions and said that He wanted all of them focused on Him. That's what this business of wholehearted love for God is all about."

"You mentioned this guy David," the young man responded. "How could he be somebody who loved God? You said he had somebody murdered and that he committed adultery. How could you consider him to be somebody who had this wholehearted love for God?"

"I'm glad you asked. You see, the important thing in having a wholehearted love for God is not human perfection. Remember what we discussed the last couple of weeks?"

"Yeah. Nobody's perfect."

"That's right. I'm not. You're not. David certainly wasn't.

"But two things made David an ideal candidate to be recognized as a man of wholehearted love for God.

"First, the major goal of his life was to be close to God and to obey Him." The older man thumbed through his stack of 3x5 cards, then pulled one out. "Here's what God said about David."

The young man took the card from his mentor's hand. "'David (son of Jesse) is a man after my own heart, for he will obey me.' (Acts 13:22) So it's that simple?" he asked. "Just do what God says?"

"That simple. Usually when God said jump, David didn't refuse or argue. He just asked 'how high?' The other thing about David was that, when he disobeyed God—and there were several times that happened in addition to the incident with Bathsheba—he admitted that he was wrong and took whatever steps were necessary to get back into fellowship with God."

"'Back into fellowship'—help me understand what you mean by that."

"God can forgive us, no matter what— if our heart is right."

"That's easy. Did you ever have disagreements with your wife? I mean, before this thing that came up a few weeks ago."

"Sure. Doesn't everybody? Sometimes it was my fault. Sometimes hers. Sometimes both of us."

"So how would you get back into fellowship?"

"Well, usually one of us would have to admit we were wrong. That's generally been a lot harder for me to do than for her. But I guess admitting you're wrong is the main thing that has to happen."

"That's exactly how it works with God. One of the verses in the Bible I use most frequently in my personal life is 1 John 1:9. It's a verse I memorized a long time ago, and I use it often—sometimes several times a day. I'd encourage you to memorize it as well."

"I guess you have it in that stack of 3x5 cards."

"Actually I don't." The older man grinned. "I memorized it before I started using cards. But here it is."

He pointed to the verse in his copy of Scripture: "But if we confess our sins to him, he can be depended on to forgive us and to cleanse us from every wrong."

"I get it. When I'm out of fellowship with God, it must always be my fault, since God is perfect."

"Exactly. So I admit to whatever wrong I've done, tell God about it, and accept His forgiveness."

"You mean, I don't have to ask Him to forgive me all over again?"

"Not really. He's already provided for your forgiveness. He just wants you to confess your wrongdoing, accept that you've been forgiven, and get back into fellowship with Him."

"Let me see if I understand this. I do something really bad like David—hire somebody to knock off my wife's boss or have an affair to get even with her—and God will still forgive me?" The young man hastily added, "Now, I'm not planning on doing anything like that, you understand."

The older man smiled. "I'm glad to hear that—I figured not. If we truly love God, we will try to obey Him. John makes that point later on in chapter 2. But the point is, God can forgive us, no matter what—if our heart is right. And by the way, 1 John 1:9 works for what we might call 'little sins' as well."

"You mean like being inconsiderate of my wife or losing my temper at my secretary?"

"Yes. Let me tell you about a couple of people I've met who, in my opinion, have shown this kind of heart for God in our day. You see, sometimes it's natural for us to feel like these kinds of attitudes were easier to practice in biblical days.

"There was a lady I met several years ago—her name was Edie. Most of her family had died, although she had one son and a daughter-in-law she saw on a regular basis. She lived alone, and I met her through a mutual friend whose life she had touched. I'd been told that Edie was a person whose friendship with Jesus Christ was as real as any human friendship we might experience. I discovered that to be true—and more. Do you remember my telling you about Moses who 'endured as seeing Him who is invisible'?"

"Sure, at our first meeting."

"Well, Edie was that kind of person. When she talked about the Lord, it was almost as though you could see Him there in the room. Prayer was a reality in her life. She was along in years, suffered a lot of pain—I think it was from arthritis or something like that. But she never let the pain sour her disposition. She had also been through a lot of personal rejection after she lost her husband. But she never became bitter. Once, I asked her how she managed to avoid bitterness. She told me, 'By staying close to the Lord.'"

The young man raised his hand, as though to ask a question in class. "Wait a minute. She sounds almost too good to be true. You don't think she was faking it, do you?"

"A valid question, but one that I can categorically answer in the negative. A colleague of mine, a minister, once said many of us seem to live by the motto 'Fake it till you make it.' But that wasn't Edie. Hers was the real thing.

"The other man—his name was Phillip—was one of my instructors in graduate school. Now, he wasn't listed in *Who's Who in America.* He wasn't noted for being the campus communicator with the greatest flair. He had never published any important books, or anything like that. But I'll tell you one thing about Phil—he was certainly a Christian who had a heart for God.

"I had a class under Phil, a senior class in biblical interpretation. His approach to interpreting drew the fire of a number of my classmates, primarily because he differed from the views espoused by some of the more popular professors. Several of the students gave him no end of grief.

"What I remember most about those classes, though, was how graciously he answered his critics—and 'critics' is probably putting it mildly. Some of those guys took some nasty potshots at him. At times I felt they were downright vicious!

"But Phil was always gracious and loving. In fact, when I think of Christ and His response to the Pharisees, I think of Phil and the way he handled those modern-day graduate students in our class.

"One other thing I'll never forget about Phil. He sometimes spoke in churches, and one weekend we invited him down to speak in the little church we were involved in. He stayed in our home, and we had a chance to get to know him. We talked about a lot of things, including the way he handled the criticism of some of my classmates.

"But that's not what impressed me the most. Our two little girls, who were toddlers, were as curious a pair as you'd ever find. He was staying in their room since we didn't have a guest room, and they were sleeping in my wife's and my room. Anyway, as it turned out, in the morning they opened their bedroom door, then came running to the breakfast table exclaiming, 'Mr. Phil's in there talking to Jesus! He's on his knees by the bed.'

"Later, when I apologized to him for the girls' interruption, he said, 'That's OK. I just have to have that time with the Lord in the morning. If I don't get it, it's like my battery isn't charged for the day.'

"You know, I had read the Bible off and on, on a regular basis since I was a teenager. But that weekend gave me a whole new perspective on the benefit of taking time every day to read. Shortly after that, I switched my time for personal Bible reading and prayer to the morning—I sometimes tended to drop off to sleep in the middle of my reading during the evenings."

The older man paused and looked at his watch. "We're just about out of time, but I sure hope you remember the difference in my friend 'Professor Phil' and some of my classmates. I'm sure if you asked them, they would have told you they loved God wholeheartedly. But looking back on it now, I think their perspective—and probably mine to a degree—was more perfectionism than wholehearted love for God. I think a lot of people today confuse those two things."

"I'm not sure I'm tracking you," said the young man.

"Just this. A perfectionist is someone who's bothered when everything isn't perfect, when things go wrong, or when everyone's views, even about the Bible, don't fit their preconceived notions. We talked about Martha earlier. I think she's a good example of a perfectionist. Martha even tried to give the Lord Jesus several pieces of advice—about

Mary and the chores, for example, and about not showing up in time to keep her brother Lazarus from dying."

Chuckling, the young man observed, "I don't suppose Jesus really needed Martha's advice, did He?"

"Not at all. But she didn't hesitate to give it. In fact, when Jesus was preparing to raise Lazarus from the dead, she was the one who warned Him not to open the tomb, insisting that the smell would be terrible, since her brother's body had already started to decompose. Now, Jesus was the Son of God, the Creator. He understood the process of decomposition better than anyone!"

Both men chuckled, and the older man added, "She just didn't—she was a perfectionist. She just didn't like the way He was running things."

"I think I'm getting your drift now. If I really love God, I'll let Him run things. If I don't like the way He's running things, maybe it's because I'm being a perfectionist."

At this point, a gentle knock on the door interrupted the conversation.

"That must be my secretary—I guess my next appointment has arrived. Let's meet here at the office next week about this time for the ball game. It's a day game, and we can leave for the ball park from here."

As the young man left, he paused beside the desk of the woman who had for many years been secretary for the man he now fondly referred to as the One Minute Christian. "A Martha inside, eh?" he whispered.

Smiling, she replied, "But not as much anymore."

7

UNCONDITIONAL
LOVE FOR PEOPLE

Let's see. Cooler with diet sodas, sunscreen, lotion—oh, and an umbrella. Sounds like you came prepared," said the man to his older companion. He was dressed in a plaid short-sleeved shirt, tan slacks, and casual shoes. He also carried an umbrella.

"We've had quite a few thundershowers recently, and I heard on the radio on the way over here that the forecast is for more showers this afternoon."

"Yeah," replied the young man, "the humidity is so thick you could almost cut it with a knife. I feel like I stepped into a sauna."

"Well, we have great seats. We'll be in the mezzanine level, almost directly behind home plate. If the weather holds, we should be in for a great game."

As the older man steered the car toward the freeway, the two men casually discussed baseball, then began talking about the forty-four-year-old right-hander who was scheduled to pitch that afternoon.

"It's incredible," said the older man, "to think about a man nearly my age competing with men who weren't even born when he started in the major leagues!"

"And just think, he's a threat to pitch a no-hitter every time he goes out there. In fact, he already has one this year!"

"That he does. Still, I remember one game last year. I was headed to the ball park to watch him pitch and got caught in a traffic jam on the way. I didn't get to the stadium until after he'd been knocked out of the game. Even the best have their bad moments."

As the two men pulled onto the freeway, they noticed a car beside the road just past the entrance ramp. Two women—one older, the other younger—were attempting to wrestle a spare tire from the rear of the car. Two small children watched from inside.

"Let's see if we can give them a hand," said the older man.

"I'm not sure we have the time," the young man replied, checking his watch. "We might be late for the start of the game—like you were last year. I'm sure someone will come along to help them."

Turning on his flashers as he pulled off in front of the disabled car, the older man insisted. "We have plenty of time—besides, have you ever been stuck with two unhappy children on a hot, steamy afternoon by the side of the road? Why don't you see if you can loosen the lug nuts? I'll wrestle the spare tire out of the trunk. Then we'll find out if their jack works."

"OK," replied the young man reluctantly as he opened his door. But inside he was steaming. *I can't believe we're taking time to do this. We're going to be late like he was last year. All the action will be over. At times I wonder if this guy is for real.*

The two men quickly jacked up the car, removed the blown tire, which appeared to be ruined, and replaced it with a spare.

"These little spares aren't designed to get you much farther than the nearest service station," said the older man as he finished tightening the last lug nut on the spare.

"But they're better than nothing," added the young man, releasing the jack so that all four wheels were once again on the ground. "Well, it looks like you ladies are ready to be on your way."

The older lady reached in her purse and took out her billfold. "Please let us pay you for your trouble."

"We wouldn't think of it," responded the older man. "It's part of our calling."

"What do you mean?" asked the younger lady, as she warned the two children not to stick their heads out the car windows.

The older man paused a moment. "Remember the story about the Good Samaritan in the Bible?" When both ladies nodded, he continued. "Ever since I came to understand what it really means to be a Christian, I've had to take the command to love my neighbor as myself seriously."

"I'm a Christian too," the older lady said, "and so is my daughter. But we don't always stop to help people by the side of the road."

"Don't get me wrong," responded the older man. "I'm not saying that's the litmus test for Christianity. There are situations in which I wouldn't think of stopping—but I might pull into the nearest service station or phone booth to call for help."

"We're sure glad you stopped to help us," said the older woman. "We could have been here for quite some time— we're supposed to meet my daughter's husband at the airport in half an hour."

"And we have an appointment at a baseball game," the young man said, opening his car door.

The two men drove for some distance in silence before the young man finally said, "Love your neighbor as yourself—wasn't that in the verses we talked about last week?"

"Yep. Right next to the command to love the Lord with all your heart. I'm glad you picked up that second commandment."

"Isn't that what used to be called the Golden Rule? The other day I heard a new version. Someone at the office said there's a modern-day Golden Rule—'He who has the gold, rules.'"

The older man laughed. "That's about what things have come to today. But I still think the rule Jesus gave works best. In fact, the way I look at it, our two major responsibilities are to love God wholeheartedly and to love people unconditionally."

"Love is not simply an emotion. It's an act of the will, a choice. It's a commitment rather than a feeling."

His young companion challenged him. "Those are our two major responsibilities? It seems to me like they're pretty broad statements. Don't you think there's more to it than that?"

Refusing to be baited into an argument, the older man replied, "I'll tell you how broad they are. According to Jesus, these are the two commandments on which all the Law and Prophets hang. In other words, they summarize the entire Old Testament."

"Well, loving some people is pretty easy to do," countered the young man. "But some people I'm just not sure I could ever love. For example, I've always considered my wife a pretty easy person to love. I still think that way even after—after what happened. But her mother? That's a different story. My wife's mother is every bad mother-in-law joke rolled into one. I think she despises me. And quite frankly, I don't think I'll ever have good feelings toward her."

The young man paused and looked over at his friend as if expecting a word of censure or rebuke. When none was forthcoming, he continued.

"Then there's my dad. We talked about him before. He was pretty cold and distant. In fact, some people might have even called him abusive. He criticized us a lot, and he was very hard on Mom. There are some things about him I respect but lots of others I don't. I'm not sure I could say I love him."

"What do you think love is?" the older man quietly asked.

"Well, " the young man measured his words, "I guess love is a feeling, a positive feeling."

Smiling, the older man took his eyes off the traffic for a moment, reached in his glove compartment, and handed the young man a small, brown New Testament. "Check out 1 Corinthians 13, beginning with verse 4."

It took the young man a few moments to find the place. Finally, he began to read.

> Love is very patient and kind, never jealous or envious, never boastful or proud, never haughty or selfish or rude. Love does not demand its own way. It is not irritable or touchy. It does not hold grudges and will hardly even notice when others do it wrong. It is never glad about injustice, but rejoices whenever truth wins out. If you love someone you will be loyal to him no matter what the cost. You will always believe in him, always expect the best of him, and always stand your ground in defending him. All the special gifts and powers from God will someday come to an end, but love goes on forever.

The older man held up his hand to signal the young man to stop reading, then asked, "Did you notice anything about *feeling* in those verses?

"Well—not exactly. Seems like it said more about what love *does*."

"That's my point exactly. Love is not simply an emotion. It's an act of the will, a choice. It's a commitment rather than a feeling. It took me a long time to—"

The older man was interrupted as he slammed on his brakes and swerved to avoid a motorist cutting in front of him on the freeway. "I guess we're not the only ones in a hurry to get to the ball game," he observed as he slowly began changing lanes in preparation for the Stadium Drive exit.

"Doesn't it bother you when people cut in front of you like that? Don't you want to get back at them?"

"I used to feel that way a lot. At times I still do. But that's what those verses you just read are all about. You see, that fellow in the car in front of us is my neighbor—at least right now he is, because he's close by. I may not know him, but I'm to choose to care about him to the same degree I care about myself. And for most of us, that's a pretty high degree."

"So you're saying that, even if I don't *feel* like loving a person—for example, my mother-in-law or my dad or even my boss—I'm loving them if I choose to behave in a loving way toward them?"

"I think that's what Paul means in 1 Corinthians," replied the older man, as he wheeled into a parking place. Dark clouds had obscured the sun, and a few large drops of rain were beginning to fall. "Let's head for the stadium. Maybe this shower will pass and the game won't get rained out."

As the two men rushed up to the nearest entrance, the raindrops began to fall faster. But when the older man handed the tickets to the middle-aged lady sitting at the turnstile, she frowned, handed them back, and said curtly, "I'm sorry, you can't come in this entrance. This entrance is for bleacher seats only. You'll have to go around to the other side of the stadium to get to the mezzanine section."

Before the older man could speak, the young man quickly said, "That's OK, ma'am. We'll try to hurry before this rain breaks loose for real." With that the two men grabbed their tickets and sprinted around the side of the stadium. Surprisingly, by the time they reached the correct gate the raindrops had just about stopped falling.

Handing their tickets to the attendant, they passed through the turnstiles and found their seats just as the lead-off hitter for the visiting team lofted a long fly ball to center field. It was caught on the warning track at the base of the fence. As the crowd applauded, the older man turned and said, "You're a quick study, aren't you?"

"What do you mean?"

"The lady back there at the ticket booth. Weren't you tempted to give her a piece of your mind—especially since no one else was around and we could have been sheltered from the rain?"

"I did think about it for a second. And I guess it would have been OK to have asked her to make an exception in our case. But I certainly didn't think it would do any good to argue with her or put her down."

As the second batter grounded sharply to the shortstop and was thrown out at first, the older man replied, "I think you're getting a handle on what this business of love is all about."

"To be honest with you though, I think it must really be hard. It was hard enough to avoid cutting down that lady back at the gate. But there are plenty of times that it's a lot harder for me to respond in a loving way to my mother-in-law or my boss. Even my wife—especially lately. What about you? You seem to have a pretty good handle on this business of loving your neighbor as yourself."

"Don't let me give you the wrong impression. It certainly isn't easy for me."

The two men were interrupted by the crack of the bat as the third hitter lined a sharp single to left field. "There goes the no hitter," said the man referred to by his companion as the One Minute Christian. "But that's OK. There's a lot of game left yet."

He returned to the subject under discussion. "What I had to learn was that I can't love people in my own strength. The apostle Paul describes love as a fruit of the Holy Spirit. That means God has to produce it in my life. It's foreign to my human nature."

The two men paused as a young couple jostled past them, carrying hotdogs, soda, and beer, stepping on random toes, spilling more than a few drops of each beverage as they passed. The young man observed wryly, "And it looks like life is just full of opportunities to exercise love."

Grinning broadly, the older man replied, "Now you're getting it."

Just at that moment, the sun broke through the clouds as the veteran pitcher struck out the visiting team's clean-up hitter with one of his patented fastballs.

Opening his cooler, the older man reached for a diet soda, then offered one to his friend. "No, thanks. I'll wait."

A few innings later, as the teams were changing sides, the young man leaned over to be heard above the crowd noise, "I've been thinking about this business of loving your neighbor as yourself. Do you think it's possible to love someone too much?"

"What's true in baseball is true in life. . . . It doesn't matter how long you've played the game of life or how experienced you might be or even how skilled you are. You still need encouragement from time to time."

"What do you mean?"

"Well, I have an aunt whose husband is an alcoholic. She really lets him take advantage of her and the kids. Sometimes he beats her up. At times he even spends money the kids need for food or school clothes on booze. My parents encouraged her to leave him—and they're certainly not big advocates of divorce—but she said she felt like she was supposed to stay and love him. What do you think?"

"Tell you what. Let's stop for a cup of coffee on the way home, and I'll give you my opinion about that situation."

During the next half-inning, the old pitcher began to struggle. He gave up a pair of singles, then walked the bases loaded. The catcher quickly trotted out to the mound and put a hand on his pitcher's shoulder.

"That's pretty remarkable, isn't it?" the young man's mentor observed. "Here's a young catcher who doesn't mind encouraging a man twice his age."

Moments later, the two men were joined on the mound by the pitching coach. The silver hair showing around the fringes of his cap suggested that he was the eldest of the three.

The young man said, "I guess it doesn't matter how much younger or older a person is—we all need encouragement."

The older man replied, "What's true in baseball is true in life. There've been times when I was struggling, and God brought people into my life—some older than me, some younger. It doesn't matter how long you've played the game of life or how experienced you might be or even how skilled you are. You still need encouragement from time to time."

"You're serious, aren't you?" responded the young man.

"Sure, why not?"

"I guess I just sort of had the impression that you were to the point where you always gave encouragement—didn't need any more yourself."

Pointing to the conference on the mound, the older companion said, "I'm sort of like our veteran pitcher. I'm experienced enough to know that I need someone—whether it's a young catcher, an older coach, or both—to help me see what I'm doing wrong and to encourage me in doing what's right.

"God has brought several people into my life at various times to meet this need. In fact, their role, which is defined in the Bible as an encourager, actually means someone called alongside to help. It's sort of the picture of an attorney who comes alongside to help as you stand before a judge to face charges.

"I remember one particularly difficult point in my life. My daughter was extremely sick, and I was under heavy pressure in my work. Two people were especially encouraging to me. One was a businessman twenty years my senior. He had very little Bible training, but he certainly had a gift of encouragement, plus a great sense of wisdom. The other was a colleague at work, fifteen years my junior, who was also gifted with a lot of wisdom and a cheerful, encouraging disposition.

"God used these two people to encourage me at a time when I easily could have given up. There've been others who have encouraged me as well. But they—"

The older man's words were drowned out by a torrent of cheers. As the two men turned their attention back to the field, they noticed that the conference on the mound had ended and that the old man had struck out the opposing team's leading hitter, ending the inning.

The young man grinned broadly, "Looks like encouragement works—at least on the baseball diamond."

"And in life," replied the older man as he pulled another diet soda from the ice chest beneath his seat and offered one to his friend. "Did you see the column by the sports editor in yesterday's paper? It seems like the old man on the mound out there is a pretty strong believer in another important aspect of encouragement—accountability."

"What do you mean?"

"*Accountability* is when you allow yourself to be answerable to someone else—letting them ask you the tough questions and committing yourself to total honesty in your answers."

"But that pitcher has probably forgotten more about pitching than anyone else associated with his team has learned. Why does he need to be accountable?"

"None of us knows everything, and none of us has complete perspective. That's why God made us with two eyes instead of one—so we'd have perspective, or depth perception. That's why we so frequently need the viewpoint of someone close to us, but different from us, so that we can gain perspective on the decisions we face—and on life itself."

"So who's the old pitcher accountable to?" the young man asked, as the two men turned their attention to the next half-inning.

"The pitching coach—the older man you saw on the mound—and the team's manager. They can ask him anything about how he's feeling, how he's pitching—and if they tell him it's time to come out, he's committed to listen to them. He may not like it, but he follows their feedback. By the way, I learned that he is accountable to his wife as well.

A couple years ago he was seriously considering retiring—perhaps even running for political office. I read where he took the time to discuss all the options with his wife and solicit her advice. The way I understand it, he told her that whenever she felt he should retire from professional baseball, he'd call it quits. She didn't feel good about his running for political office, even though a lot of his friends felt he'd be very successful. So he took her advice and stuck with his baseball career."

The home team had been quickly retired, and the old man was walking slowly back to the mound. The young spectator turned to his mentor. "Are you accountable to someone?"

"I sure am. To my wife and to several men, some of whom are close friends, some ministry associates. In fact, there's a group of us who practice accountability in such things as how we handle sexual temptations, whether we're working too much, whether we're spending enough time with our families, even whether we're spending time in the Word and prayer every day."

The young man thought, *That's the last thing I want anyone doing. I don't need that kind of grief.* "Don't you resent that?" he asked out loud.

"Actually, no. I've found it keeps me on my toes. Plus, I consider it a positive motivation. I remember reading somewhere once that the unexamined life is not worth living."

The young man looked around the stadium at the thousands of people enjoying a holiday afternoon of baseball. His gaze returned to the old pitcher standing on the mound, perspiration pouring from his brow, staring in to get the sign from the catcher. "And he's accountable to the catcher for every pitch he throws, isn't he?"

"Well, he does reserve the right to shake off a sign occasionally, but generally speaking, he is."

The young man turned to look at the man sitting next to him. He noticed the gray at his temples, the laugh lines, the crinkled corners of his kindly eyes. *Maybe I really do need to be accountable to someone. It seems to be working for a couple of pretty successful people.*

"Could I be accountable to you?" he asked.

"Only if you're willing for me to ask you the toughest of questions about any area of your life—and only if you'll remember that I'd be asking you, not to trip you up, but because I care about you."

"That's what I want."

"And one more thing. You need to feel free to ask me the tough questions too."

"I don't know about that. But—if you say so."

"I say so."

All too soon the game was over. The two men made their way to the car and headed back down the freeway.

"The old pitcher didn't win today, but he put in a respectable performance," the young man observed.

"Six innings, and only a couple of earned runs against him—I'd say that's not bad for someone his age. Ready for that cup of coffee?"

"Sure, I'd just about forgotten. But I do want to know about this business of loving your neighbor and if it's possible to love too much."

They found a coffee shop and were seated in a corner booth. The older man ordered coffee, the young man iced tea. "How familiar are you with the story of the Good Samaritan?" the older man asked.

"I think I remember it from my Sunday school days. Some guy was assaulted by robbers and left for dead on a highway somewhere. Didn't a bunch of people pass by him after he was attacked?"

"Not a *group* of people. Just a couple are mentioned, but they were pretty important people—a priest and an Levite. A priest was like a clergyman today. The Levites were in charge of the activities at the Temple—worship, sacrifice, things like that.

"But the third person to come along was a Samaritan. Now Samaritans were the outcasts of their day. They suffered a lot of discrimination. People just didn't have any so-cial contact with them. But this Samaritan saw the injured man and cared for him. The Bible said he had compassion, bandaged the man's wounds, let him ride on his own don-key on the way to an inn, and paid for his care."

"Sounds like he showed his love by his actions."

"Precisely. Some time ago I was studying the story again and something struck me—there were some things he didn't do."

"Real love is action—things like patience, kindness, gentleness. It includes encouragement and accountability. It sacrifices, but it has limits."

"I'm not sure I understand what you mean. I thought your point was all the things he did do to help this injured man."

The older man smiled. "One of the things I've noticed about the Bible is that sometimes it speaks the loudest when it's silent. I finally realized that the story Jesus told about this man could help me understand something a lot of people are puzzled about today—where love ends and where what is called 'codependency' begins."

"Ah, codependency. I just finished reading a book on the subject. I suspect it's what my aunt has been doing for my uncle. Codependency isn't in the Bible, is it? You're the One Minute Christian, the man with the answers. Tell me if the Bible says anything about loving too much."

The young man's mentor shook his head. "Not in so many words. But I've sort of made a mental list of the things the Good Samaritan *didn't* do. He didn't interrupt his trip—or maybe I should say he *only* interrupted his trip, but he didn't cancel it. He was willing to be interrupted to help this man at his point of need. But he didn't give up his ultimate purpose."

"He did spend money on the guy. That's a pretty hefty commitment."

"But he didn't commit to supporting the man for the rest of his life," the older man replied. He didn't offer him permanent financial support. Didn't even take the man with him. He was willing to spend what was needed to take care of the immediate situation. Evidently, according to the Bible, that was the man's limit."

"And Jesus said he showed mercy."

"Exactly. And he told us to go and do likewise."

"Go and do likewise," the young man echoed. "But it's OK to have limits." He looked up at the older man. "You know there were a couple of guys who helped us a few months ago when my wife and I were driving back from a weekend at the beach. I ran completely out of gas. You know, that German machine I drive never gives me any problems—unless I forget to put fuel in it. I had thought I would be able to make the next town—but I didn't. A couple of fellows in a pick-up truck came by—they must have been Good Samaritans. They drove twenty miles out of their way to the nearest service station and back. Actually paid for the gasoline themselves. I offered to reimburse them, even pay them for helping. The wouldn't hear of it. Said they were glad to help. I guess you'd call them Good Samaritans. They invested time—and even money. And they'll never get anything back from us. Sounds like they were practicing unconditional love."

The young man paused. "I think I've learned some things about unconditional love for people today."

"And what have you learned?"

"I've learned that real love is action—things like patience, kindness, gentleness. It includes encouragement and accountability. It sacrifices, but it has limits. But I'm sure there's a lot more I need to learn about love."

"Don't we all," replied the older man as he picked up the check, "but that's what life is all about."

8

BE YOURSELF

Have you seen him?" the man sometimes referred to as the One Minute Christian asked his secretary as he walked toward his office, coffee in hand.

"No," replied the slim, cheerful, woman. "He's twenty minutes late now."

"And it's not like him to be late," the middle-aged man replied, running his fingers through his somewhat thinning hair. "He impresses me as the kind of person who's generally punctual—maybe something has come up."

At that moment the door opened and the young man, looking a bit more disheveled than usual, entered. He was wearing old slacks and a pullover golf shirt.

Placing his freshly poured mug of coffee on the corner of his secretary's desk, the older man greeted his colleague warmly. "We were beginning to get concerned about you. I was about to ask Debra if she had your car phone number."

"It wasn't the traffic. I almost didn't come today. In fact, as you can see by how I'm dressed, I didn't go to the office. I decided to take the day off. Listen, it's time for me to stop taking up so much of your time. I'm sure you have other things more pressing that you need to be doing. So I thought I'd just check in with you, then get out of your hair."

"Hold the phone, now. Come on in the office, and let's talk about it. Debra, could you bring our friend a cup of coffee?"

"Two sugars, one cream. Right?"

"You certainly are observant. OK. But I won't take up much of your time today. I promise."

"Like I've told you before, my schedule is my own. If I choose to spend time with you, that's my call. I've been a grownup for quite some time now. I'm certainly old enough to know what I have time to do."

Slowly, almost reluctantly, the young man entered the office of the older man and sat down in the chair he was offered. Waiting until his secretary brought the coffee, he gently closed the door, then sat down next to his friend.

After pausing for a moment, he asked, "Can you tell me what's bothering you?"

Too quickly the young man replied, "Nothing's bothering me. I just think it's time for me to quit wasting so much of your time. I'm not feeling too well today—didn't get a lot of sleep last night. I guess I'm exhausted. Maybe it's time we just called these meetings to a halt."

The older man looked in the face of the younger colleague he had grown to appreciate. "If you're not feeling so good about yourself, it's OK to say so. If there's something bothering you—something you haven't handled very well—that's OK too. And I hope you remember that if there's anything I've said or done that's bothered you, it's always OK to bring that up."

"No. It's nothing like that. Nothing you've said or done. It's—it's just me! Every time I think I'm getting a handle on things, I blow it again. Yesterday at the office, I didn't have a report ready my boss had asked for—and he was plenty upset. Apparently the people at corporate are on his case. I think they're worried about the possibility of a hostile takeover, and he needed the figures he had asked me to get together. I really blew it, and he threatened to have Herman get the stuff together for him next time if I couldn't produce soon enough. Herman's a young shark. He would like nothing better than to take over my position and cut me out of the picture."

The words seemed to pour from the young man like raindrops from a thunderhead. "Then, when I got home last night, I took things out on my wife. She didn't deserve it. She hasn't been feeling well—she's had a sinus infection for several days. On top of all that, she has a doctor's appointment coming up soon to look into something we've both been a little concerned about for a while.

"Last night she tried to ask me what was bothering me—sort of like you did just now—but I really blew up at her. Told her it was all her fault. That if she were more supportive of me, I'd do a better job at work. I even brought up her affair with the guy at the museum. I had promised her I wouldn't do that ever again, but I did. She didn't deserve it, and I felt miserable afterwards. We didn't speak for the rest of the evening. My parents used to carry on like that, and I promised myself we wouldn't do it—but I've lost it with her several times this past week."

The young man paused to take a sip of his coffee. The older man asked him, "Are you telling me you really don't like yourself very well?"

Setting his cup down on the conference table, the young man raised both arms in a shrug of helplessness. "I guess that's it. I think if you put everything in a nutshell, that would be it. I just don't like the person I am. By the way, I meant to say 'thank you' for taking me to the ball game. I really enjoyed it. It was the first time I've had fun in quite a while."

"I figured a BMW in the garage, a good stock portfolio, and a handful of gold and platinum credit cards would mark me as a success. . . . But I just don't feel very successful. I keep asking myself, 'Is this all there is?'"

"Actually, from what you've already told me this morning, I'd say you're ready for my next two rules: Be yourself; and have fun. Let's start with the first one—be yourself—

since that seems to be the area that's hard for you right now."

"To be honest with you, I'm a little confused about who I am right now."

"In what way?"

"Well, I've been confused about who I am and what I'm supposed to think about myself for quite a while. When I was a kid, I was pretty motivated in school and in sports— you know, all the usual things people in high school get into.

"Then I got to college and there were people who were a lot better than me, both academically and in athletics. I began to have doubts about whether I could cut it. I worked pretty hard in college but never did much in sports. Had to drop out of football, played varsity basketball one year till I hurt my knee. When I finished college, I decided business was the way to success, so I went after the old MBA. I figured a BMW in the garage, a good stock portfolio, and a handful of gold and platinum credit cards would mark me as a success. Now I have the Beamer, the cards, and a pretty fair portfolio too. Nice house, beautiful wife, the whole bit. But I just don't feel very successful. I keep asking myself, 'Is this all there is?' I don't feel too good about myself either—"

The monologue trailed off, and the older man asked, "You mentioned being confused about how you feel about yourself—said a couple of things had confused you this past week. Tell me about them."

A puzzled look came across the young man's face. *Is this guy a mind reader? He always seems to ask the right questions.* Aloud he said, "Well, we had this management seminar—they flew us down to corporate for a day, brought in this heavy hitting motivational speaker. He told us we really needed to crank up how we feel about ourselves— you know, think positively, the whole bit. According to this character, the biggest problem in the universe is that most of us haven't realized that we're really a part of God. He said all of us, him included, had to raise our level of self-consciousness to the point where we recognize that God is within us. It sounded a lot like what I'd been learning from meeting with you, but it was kind of different too. He didn't say anything about Jesus, for example. He just kept harping on thinking more positively about ourselves, getting rid of all negative thoughts. Flushing them from our minds. Self-actualization, I think he called it. Sounded pretty impressive.

"Then this past weekend, we went to visit my wife's family. Went with them to this new church they've been attending, and the pastor's sermon seemed to be just the opposite. He sort of preached on the words to a song—something about such a worm as I. In fact, I think that was the point of his message—that we're supposed to look at ourselves as worms. Maybe I didn't hear him exactly right, but he seemed to be saying that you ought to think totally negatively about yourself. Never have any positive thoughts about yourself. Just think about God all the time. He said you're supposed to put Jesus first, others second, and yourself last, if at all. He said that's the way we're to have joy in life."

Taking a sip from his own rapidly-cooling cup of coffee, the older man rolled his chair back so he could reach the surface of his desk. He picked up his copy of Scripture, began thumbing through its pages, then handed it to his young companion. "Here are a couple of the most well-known verses in the Bible. Romans 12:1 and 2. Read them and tell me if they're familiar to you."

> And so, dear brothers, I plead with you to give your bodies to God. Let them be a living sacrifice, holy—the kind he can accept. When you think of what he has done for you, is this too much to ask? Don't copy the behavior and customs of this world, but be a new and different person with a fresh newness in all you do and think. Then you will learn from your own experience how his ways will really satisfy you.

Looking up at his companion, the young man nodded. "I remember those verses. When I was attending that col-

lege Bible study group for a while, I actually tried to memorize them. Everybody else in the group was, and I sort of
went along with them. Almost said them perfect once."

"That's good. Now what about the next verse? Verse 3?"

The young man looked down at the page, found his
place, then resumed reading: "As God's messenger I give
each of you God's warning: Be honest in your estimate of
yourselves, measuring your value by how much faith God
has given you."

The young man paused, a puzzled expression on his
face. "I don't think I've ever heard that verse before, or even
seen it."

"Probably not," the gray-haired man replied, reaching
into the pocket of his Day Timer to remove a wrinkled 3x5
card. The young man noticed that this particular card was
green. Handing the card to him, the older man said, "This is
the version I memorized that verse in."

The young man read it: "'For I say, through the grace
given me, to everyone who is among you, not to think of
himself more highly than he ought to think, but to think soberly, as God has dealt to each one a measure of faith'
(NKJV). It does talk about thinking about yourself, doesn't
it?"

"Precisely. Now think with me for a minute. Does it say
not to think of yourself at all?"

"Well, actually, it doesn't say 'Don't ever think of yourself.' It just sort of tells *how* to think about yourself."

"That's what I'm getting at," replied the One Minute
Christian. "I've studied both the Old and New Testaments
pretty carefully over the years. I have yet to find a verse any-
where that says, 'Don't ever think of yourself.' You know,
God made us. He knows us a lot better than anybody else—
and He knows it's natural for us to think about ourselves.
But I do think this verse recognizes that we generally have
more problems with thinking highly of ourselves than with
thinking too lowly of ourselves."

"You mean like pride? I've always heard it's one of the

seven deadly sins. In fact, that pastor this past weekend labeled it the most dangerous sin of all."

"I'd probably agree with him on that. But I'm convinced from my personal experience, and from talking with professional counselors, that what may seem like pride or even arrogance is often a result of feelings of inferiority."

"Sounds like Herman—the guy at work I was telling you about. He seems so arrogant, so brash—comes on like gangbusters, trying to let everybody know how much he knows about everything. He doesn't even attempt to be subtle. Maybe he's insecure. Could be he even feels inferior."

"Probably so," the older man replied. "By the way, did you ever learn to ride a bicycle?"

"Sure. When I was a kid. But what's that got to do with how I think about myself? Unless you're going to tell me that falling off a bicycle causes poor self-esteem."

The older man chuckled. "That's not what I had in mind. What I'm driving at is that learning to ride a bicycle can be summed up in one word—balance. And in that sense it's a lot like life. You've heard me talk about balance before."

As the young man nodded, his companion continued. "You see, I think most of us have a tendency to go to one extreme or the other. Some people, like the seminar speaker you heard last week, spend all their time talking about how positively we need to think about ourselves. In the process, they seem to almost elevate man to the position of a deity. I've even known of some preachers who tend to take that position.

"But I know a lot of Christians who take the other extreme. They tell us that what we really need to do is almost hate ourselves. Spend all our time focusing on what lowly, miserable sinners we are. I've probably heard that 'worm' business you were talking more than a hundred times.

"But I'm convinced the Bible doesn't really tell us we're supposed to think of ourselves as worms. I looked up all the references to that word in the Bible once. Used a concordance. Most of them were Old Testament references to the nation of Israel—statements like 'Fear not, you worm Jacob.' Most of them actually seemed to suggest that, while Israel viewed herself as a worm and while her enemies may have seen her that way as well, God's plan was to elevate those people to a much higher status."

"You have to balance these two things out: We were created in God's image, but every one of us has fallen into sin."

Rising from his seat, the older man walked over to the markerboard, erased a series of notes from an earlier session, then drew a triangle with a line across the top. "What do you see?"

"I'm not sure."

He picked up a different colored marker and drew stick figures at either end of the horizontal line. "Now what do you see now?"

"It looks like a seesaw—what we used to call a teeter-totter."

"Probably the best, most simple, example of balance in human experience. Maybe even a better illustration than the bicycle. After all, who hasn't ridden a seesaw at some time or other? Now, on this side we have evidence for feeling positive about ourselves." The older man wrote on the board, then moved to the side, allowing the young man to see the word he had written: "CREATED."

"You see, God created each one of us as a unique individual, as different from everyone else as snowflakes. No two of us are just alike, not even identical twins. In fact, the Bible says that the very hairs of our head are numbered. That statement has become special to me, because I'm beginning to lose a few of mine." He touched the thinning spot on the back of his head, then resumed his writing. When he finished, he moved aside again, allowing the young man to see the word on the other side of the teeter-totter: "FALLEN."

Returning to his seat, the older man said, "The problem, as you know, is that we chose to rebel against God, to go our own way. We were created in God's image, but we shattered the image when we fell. The theologians have a fancy term for where we are today—they call it total depravity."

"The preacher last Sunday used that term several times. I've always thought of that as only applying to mass murderers—criminals like Charles Manson or maybe dictators like Hitler or Saddam Hussein. Don't most of us have some good in us?"

"I suppose you could say we all have some good in us—in one sense. But remember last week when we stopped on the way to the ball game to help those ladies change their tire? I grew up next door to a man who seemed to spend a lot of his time going out of his way to help people with flat tires and other automotive problems. But he made it clear to everyone that he wasn't a Christian—didn't have any use for God or Christianity—but he did a lot of humanitarian things. He even gave money to charity. He was a long-haul truck driver, sort of a self-made man—in business for himself. But his big deal was that he didn't want to be beholden to God or anybody.

"Now here's the problem. You have to balance these two things out: We were created in God's image, but every one of us has fallen into sin. And, as you've already learned, none of us can do enough good deeds to counter the sins we've committed."

"That's why Christ had to pay for our sins."

"Exactly. He did for us what we could never do for ourselves, and I think that's why He spent so much time emphasizing balance in the way we're to think about ourselves. Let's take a look at that verse again." Pointing to the 3x5 card he said, "Let's list some important points about what this verse says."

Turning to the blackboard he wrote:

Romans 12:3
1.
2.
3.
4.

"Now let's see if we can pick out the important things Paul said about how we're to think about ourselves. What's the first thing you notice?"

The young man carefully studied the verse in front of him, then looked up at his older companion. "Well, like I said before, he didn't say, 'Don't think about yourself at all.'"

"Good." He wrote on the board, "It's OK to think about yourself." Drawing a line through the word OK, he wrote "natural." He repeated both the words he had written. "It's natural and OK to think about yourself. What else?"

"I guess you might say that the biggest danger is to think too highly of yourself. After all, he mentioned that first."

In the second space the older man wrote, "Danger #1: Overinflated opinion of self."

Turning to his companion, he asked, "Is that what you're saying?"

"I think so. And it makes sense doesn't it? Maybe that's where the guy who was doing the seminar was coming from. You know, thinking of himself more highly than he should."

"It seems like that's pretty common today. What's next?"

The young man continued to look at the verse. "Well, the next part says to think soberly. What does that mean? Seems like he's changing subjects. I mean, why would he mention something about not getting drunk in this verse?"

"You're asking the right questions. But, actually, the word *soberly* isn't limited to not being 'under the influence.'

One alternate meaning is 'to think realistically or seriously.' It's the idea of using sound judgment."

"Why does he use that word here? What's the point?"

The One Minute Christian drew a circle around the stick drawing of the seesaw on his markerboard. "It's that thing of balance again. Undoubtedly our biggest problem is thinking too highly of ourselves. But there are quite a number of us who struggle with feelings of inferiority. Maybe we've had critical parents who put us down. Maybe we've been abused. Some of us have been emotionally or physically trashed as children. We grew up with a huge load of inferiority. We don't see ourselves as having any value at all. In fact, I suspect the pastor you heard last Sunday may even struggle from those kinds of feelings himself. I think it's pretty common among people who spend a lot of time telling others to think of themselves as 'nothings.'"

"Feelings of inferiority—I guess I struggle with those a lot myself," the young man said. "I'm not sure why. My parents were somewhat critical at times—especially my dad— but they didn't abuse us. Still, I guess maybe I never quite felt like I was good enough. That's why I felt like I needed to quit coming to see you. Inside, I kept thinking I just didn't measure up. I thought there were better people you could spend your time with. People who would be more likely to succeed."

Smiling, the older man walked over to the window and opened the curtain. "Look at that crowd of kids at recess." A group of children were rushing about the playground engaging in various kinds of recreation.

"I want to tell you about a man every one of those kids knows about. A man who probably had more reasons to feel inferior than almost anybody of his era. At the age of seven, he and his family were evicted from their home. Humiliated, they had to find a new place to live. Two years later, his mother died. As a child, he was forced to work to help pay the family's bills. At twenty-three he went into business with a friend. Three years later, the friend died, leaving a sizable debt that took years to repay.

"Throughout his youth he felt awkward and shy in personal relationships—especially with girls. He was twenty-eight when he finally found the courage to ask his long-time girlfriend to marry him. She refused. Later, he married another woman, but the marriage was unhappy. Three of the couple's four son's died before reaching adulthood.

"The young man decided to go into politics. Twice he ran for congressional office. Each time he was defeated. After finally winning on his third try, he lost his re-election bid two years later. At forty-five he ran for the U.S. Senate—and lost. Two years later, he sought the nomination for vice president of the United States. He lost again. Then he ran for the Senate again."

"And lost?" the young man asked.

"Again."

"Sounds like enough to drive somebody to a nervous breakdown."

"As a matter of fact, that's exactly what happened. But in the fall of 1860, this man was elected president of the United States. He was Abraham Lincoln."

A look of surprise on his face, the young man responded, "I never knew all that. That's almost impossible to believe. I mean—you told me a couple weeks ago how he forgave that guy who was out to get him. I always figured Lincoln must have been one of the most self-assured people who ever lived."

"Quite the contrary. Lincoln probably spent most of his life struggling with feelings of inferiority. But he didn't let that keep him from persisting. Not only did he become president, but I recently read a poll of historians who listed Lincoln as our country's all-time most respected president.

"Let me tell you about another national leader who was as respected in his day as Lincoln was in his—Moses."

"Right. The ten plagues on Egypt and the parting of the Red Sea."

"Actually, before all that happened, Moses got into a big argument with God about whether or not he should be the one to lead the Israelites out of Egypt."

"You're kidding." The young man leaned forward as his older companion flipped through the pages of his copy of Scripture, finally locating the third chapter of Exodus.

"What really matters is not how good we are or how impressive our background or our credentials. . . . What really counts is being connected to God. He's the one who actually makes us somebody."

"You see, Moses spent forty years in the court of Pharaoh, the King of Egypt. Then he spent the next forty years as an obscure shepherd on the back side of the Arabian Desert. At that point, no one—including Moses—expected him to be tapped by God to lead the Israelites out of captivity. But that's exactly what happened. It says God appeared to Moses in the form of a burning bush and told him, 'You are the person I want to lead my people Israel out of Egypt.' It was at that point that Moses began to argue with God.

"Here was Moses' first objection. 'But I am not the person for a job like that!'"

"I probably would have said the same thing."

"Look at God's reply."

The young man read, "Then God told him, 'I will certainly be with you—'"

"Stop right there. That's the most important point in this entire argument. The real issue wasn't how good Moses was—how sharp or how effective a leader. Not even how strongly Moses believed in himself, or how much potential he had. What counted was, God promised to be with him. Moses was somebody because God was with him."

"Didn't you say he continued to argue?"

The older man smiled and nodded, "That's exactly what he did. First, he tried to tell God that the Israelites wouldn't believe that God had appeared to him. So God gave Moses a miraculous sign—He caused his shepherd's staff to turn into a snake when he threw it on the ground.

"But Moses wasn't through arguing. He said, 'I'm just not a good speaker.' So God asked, 'Who makes mouths?' Then He promised to be with Moses and to help him say what needed to be said."

"So did that persuade him?"

"As a matter of fact, no. At that point, Moses actually had the audacity to say, 'Lord, please! Send someone else.'"

"I think if I were God, I would have been pretty mad at Moses by that time."

"He was! God had already told Moses that he was somebody because He—God—was with him. He promised to authenticate His message and to give Moses strength to communicate it. But Moses was like a lot of us. Just a little too stubborn for his own good."

"Did he ever go ahead and do what God told him to do?"

"Finally," replied the gray-haired man. "I think Moses had to realize something that's important to us today. What really matters is not how good we are or how impressive our background or our credentials. It doesn't really matter how many gold or platinum credit cards we carry or whether we have an impressive degree from a prestigious school. What really counts is being connected to God. He's the one who actually makes us somebody."

At this point the conversation was interrupted by a knock at the door. The secretary stuck her head in. "Your visitors from Houston have arrived."

The young man hastily stood to his feet, almost spilling his coffee in the process. "Guess I better be going then."

"Not at all," replied the older man. "Not at all. In fact, I want you to meet my friend Robert. He's one of the shyest people you'd ever meet, but he wrote a book that's helped literally thousands of people with the very problem we've been talking about. Poor self-esteem."

"Are you sure I won't be interrupting?"

"Not at all. Debra, show them in please."

The older man introduced his young colleague to his guests, then invited everyone to take a seat. Indicating the taller of the two visitors, he said, "Robert's in town to present a seminar tonight on the subject of personal growth and self-esteem from a biblical perspective. It's called 'Search for Significance.' I wanted you to meet him because he developed his material out of his own struggles in this area. Isn't that right, Robert?"

Gently nodding a head covered with reddish-brown hair, the visitor looked at the young man with sparkling green eyes. "I probably felt as badly about myself as anybody ever did. You see, I grew up in a small town in Oklahoma. I was terribly shy. Felt extremely insecure. Most of the people around me didn't like me much, and I didn't like me too well, either. I was very self-conscious. Finally, I wound up in Viet Nam, piloting a helicopter gunship. But I still struggled with who I was."

After pausing, the visitor continued, "I began to study two areas. The Bible and the field of counseling. I came to realize that to a great degree probably every one of us struggles with bad feelings about who we are. That's why so many of us fall into trying to prove our self-worth by achievement of some kind or other."

The young man's mentor picked up the conversation. "In his book, Robert calls that 'the performance trap'—it's one of several false beliefs about personal significance. Another is the approval addict."

"What's that?"

The visitor responded. "That's trying to prove our significance by gaining the acceptance and approval of others. I really struggled with that one quite a bit as well. I was convinced I was a nobody unless I could win the approval of people around me. But I never seemed to be able to get it."

"So what finally cured you?" asked the young man.

"Well, I'm not sure you'd call it a cure. I think what happened was that my thinking was rearranged. The Bible calls it the renewing of your mind. I finally came to the place where I learned to base my self-worth on the love and acceptance and approval I have from God in Jesus Christ instead of on my performance—or my ability to please other people."

"That's what the One Minute Christian has been trying to tell me today—but it's been hard for me to accept."

Smiling, the visitor responded, "The One Minute Christian, eh? I'm familiar with his book, but I didn't know that's what he'd started calling himself."

Embarrassed the young man quickly responded, "He hasn't—I just started referring to him that way."

"Oh, I see." The visitor continued. "You know, these things are really hard for all of us to accept. Those false beliefs are pretty thoroughly ingrained in us. Usually from early in childhood."

The young man thought, *These guys must go to the same school. They're all hitting me with the same hammer. But I'm beginning to think they must be right.*

"I wish I could attend your seminar," he said, "but I have a previous commitment, a business appointment. I think this conversation has been really helpful, though. But I need to get going now. I think I'll head back to the office. I'm glad I had a chance to meet you men."

"Let me give you a copy of Robert's book," said the older Christian as he reached for one of his bookshelves. "I think you'll find it helpful."

"And I'll try to remember that it's not so much who I am or what I do, it's *who* I know," replied the young man, pointing his index finger upward as he exited his mentor's office.

9

DON'T WORRY, BE PRAYERFUL

The following Monday, light rain was falling from leaden skies. The man sometimes called the One Minute Christian turned into the parking lot of his office. Noticing the shiny, European automobile occupying a visitor's spot in the parking lot, he wondered why his young friend had arrived so early.

As he pulled into his parking space, the young man jumped out of his car and raced over before the older gentleman could open his door. Instead of his usual, neatly-pressed suit, shirt, and tie, the young man was dressed in a wrinkled sport shirt, jeans, and a light jacket.

"I've got something I need to tell you about," he said frantically.

"Come into the office. Let's get out of the rain," the older man responded as he locked his car door.

When the two men had entered the office, the older man said, "I'll make us a pot of coffee, then you can tell me all about it."

"Please, let's not take the time for that. I need to tell you about what happened. I didn't sleep a wink last night." The knuckles of his hands were white as he pressed his fingers together.

Gently, the older man put a hand on his shoulder, "Come on in the office and sit down. Let's talk about it."

"I—don't know—what we're going to do," the young man said, his voice tense and halting. "Yesterday, the doctors found a lump in my wife's breast—just when things were beginning to get better for us again. Cancer runs in her family. One of her aunts died with breast cancer last year. In fact, she's lost several of her family members to cancer of one kind or another."

"I'm sorry to hear that. How's your wife handling it?"

"Better than I am! She doesn't seem nearly as worried. She's even tried to encourage *me*, especially when I got all uptight about how much insurance coverage we had. I was rummaging through the house, throwing papers here and there, trying to find out whether we had a cancer rider on our hospitalization insurance—or whether we needed one. It was too late in the day to call our insurance agent. I was really embarrassed that she had to calm me down.

"I decided not to go into work today. I'm so distracted I probably wouldn't be able to get anything done anyway. It's a good thing I had another personal day I could take. But I don't think my boss will be too happy about this. There's another big report due tomorrow, and I'm a little worried about that."

With a twinkle in his eye, the older Christian replied, "Well, you're certainly not the first person who was worried about worrying too much. In fact, I think worrying is one of the most common things we do in life. I've found that worry and fear usually go hand-in-hand. I had planned to talk to you today about having fun—but let's put that discussion on the back burner till we tackle these worries of yours.

"By the way, did you know that Jesus had a lot to say about worry? He probably gave the best discussion on how to live worry free ever given."

Shuffling papers that were stacked high on his desk, he said, "I'm sure my Bible is here somewhere. Give me a second to find it." For a moment, he paused, looked at his friend, and grinned. "Well, maybe I left it at home. I used to worry about that sort of thing. But I guess we'll just have to use my spare."

Pulling a relatively new Bible off one of his bookshelves, he invited his friend to take his familiar seat at the conference table in the corner of the office. Pulling back the shade to allow what outside light there was to filter into the room, he said, "It's pretty glum-looking out there, but I like the natural light anyway."

The two men sat down and the older man directed his friend's attention to the book of Matthew. "This is called the Sermon on the Mount. It's one of Jesus' most famous sermons."

"I think you had me look at these verses before. Yeah, I'm sure you did. This is where He says, 'Don't worry.'"

"You're right. We did look at these verses before. But I don't think it will hurt to look at them again, especially since this is the main place where Jesus discusses the subject of worry and anxiety. I discovered that, out of the twenty-five or so times the word for worry is used in the New Testament, about a fourth of them are found here. As you may remember, the word itself actually has the idea of being distracted or divided in your thinking. It describes any concern, whether legitimate or unnecessary. It seems that anxiety distracts our attention away from other things."

"That's what I'm struggling with right now," said the young man. "Not being able to concentrate. It seems pretty bad."

"Actually, at times anxiety can be good. The apostle Paul used the word several times to describe his concern for other people and when he referred to Timothy's concern for the churches he served. But most of the time, the word has a negative connotation."

"That's the impression I got from those verses. It kept saying, 'Do not be anxious,' and I'd like not to be anxious. But how do I stop?"

"Well, let's start right here in the Sermon on the Mount," the older man suggested. "I think we'll find some keys to worry-free living. Now, worry is a little bit like fat calories—we don't completely eliminate them, but we can take some steps to minimize them. I don't know that any of us will be able to live completely worry free, but we can certainly cut our worries down to a minimum. The first key is that we need to gain insight into anxiety's hidden root.

Did you notice the kinds of things Jesus told His listeners to stop worrying about?"

"I don't remember." Scanning the verses again, the young man offered some suggestions. "Food, clothing— sounds like the basic necessities of life."

"Precisely. Most of us probably worry about making a living or just making ends meet about as much as anything. Especially with the impact of the recession.

"The other thing we typically worry about is keeping up with the Joneses. Did you notice the verse that said, 'Why be like the heathen? For they take pride in all these things and are deeply concerned about them'?"

"Yeah, I wondered about that. Do you think people sought after status symbols in those days like we do today —designer clothes, cars like BMWs and Mercedes? Maybe they had designer togas, or foreign-bred camels or donkeys."

The older man laughed. "They probably had some kinds of status symbols. By the way, I know you drive a BMW. I don't think He's condemning certain brands of cars or clothes. I think the point is not to let those things distract us from what really matters in life. But there's something we need to track down first. See if you can find the hidden root."

"When we lack *faith, we rely on ourselves and therefore worry; when we* have *faith, however, we are empowered to rely on God instead of ourselves."*

For the third time, the young man looked through the verses in front of him. "I'm still not sure I see what you're driving at. I can't figure out the hidden root."

"Was there anything that sort of jumped out at you as you read the verses? Anything sort of pointed or personal?"

"Well, not exactly. Maybe that phrase about 'men of little faith.' But I'm not sure what that has to do with worrying about making ends meet."

"Ah, it has everything to do with it. That's the hidden root of anxiety. Let me tell you how I came to understand what this means.

"When I was in college, I drove a Volkswagen—you know, one of those little bugs?"

Both men chuckled. "You mean those things that had a motor that sounded like a sewing machine?"

"Sounds like you had one yourself," the older man replied.

When the young man shook his head, his mentor continued. "Those cars were really great as far as gasoline mileage went. And they ran well too. They just had one problem. They didn't have enough horsepower.

"Sometimes I'd try to get into traffic at a busy intersection, or pass another car on the highway—back then there weren't so many freeways. A lot of the roads I drove on were two-lane highways, where you often had to pass trucks and slower traffic going uphill. You could put that car to the floorboard, but about all it would do is cause the engine to whine at a higher pitch. It did almost nothing to increase the speed. That engine just had too few horses. In a sense, that's what I think Jesus is telling his listeners here. They're worried because their faith doesn't have enough 'horsepower.'"

"How can faith have horsepower?"

"It isn't that faith actually has horsepower or energy. It's that, when we *lack* faith, we rely on ourselves and therefore worry; when we *have* faith, however, we are empowered to rely on God instead of ourselves. You see, most of us feel responsible to take care of a lot of things, like I'm sure you feel responsible to take care of your wife, provide for your family. And today we live in sort of a do-it-yourself, take-care-of-it-yourself society anyway. I think the reason Jesus was telling these people to quit worrying so much about the basics of life wasn't that He intended for them to stop working. They needed to do what they *could* do, but they also needed to leave everything else up to Him."

"So how does that relate to Suzi and me, and this possibility of cancer?"

"Let me put it like this. I think it's important for you and your wife to do everything you possibly can—then leave the rest up to God. That's what faith is all about. The second key to worry-free living is to make the main thing the main thing—in other words, to establish proper priorities."

"Now you're talking my language," the young man interrupted enthusiastically. "I've attended a number of workshops and seminars designed to help us prioritize. I think developing priorities is one of the most important things we can do, but I'm not sure it's a solution for worry. In fact, if anything, prioritizing sometimes causes me more anxiety. Especially when I try to juggle all the responsibilities and projects I have at work."

The older man smiled. "It's interesting that you relate priorities to work. That's a very common thing I've observed among businessmen. And certainly they can help us manage our workload more effectively. But the priority Jesus is talking about extends well beyond the workplace."

Pointing to the Bible in front of him, he continued. "Take a look at this—see what it says about priority."

The young man looked down and read, "'And he will give them to you if you give him first place in your life and live as he wants you to.' This is the verse you explained to me the first time we got together—when you were talking about living life one day at a time. I wasn't even a Christian then—I realize that now. Maybe I'm in a better position to understand what He's saying now. But I'm still not sure I get the point. He's not saying put church attendance first is He?"

The older man gently shook his head. "Not exactly. I think church attendance is only a small part of the equation. You may remember that giving Him first place involves His right to rule our lives—to have a say-so over our decisions.

Living as He wants us to involves applying His standards to the way we've lived."

"I'm still not sure how all this affects my life. Could you elaborate?"

"Sure. Let me give you an 'instant replay.' There are times when all of us have to choose between what's important to God and what's important to us. This statement suggests that we put every decision, every activity, through the grid of His authority and righteous standards.

"Here's how it affects me, for example. If I'm faced with a decision about scheduling, perhaps a work project or some other activity, or a business opportunity, based on this principle, I evaluate it for two things. First, does it violate any clear-cut commands of Scripture? Does it force me to say yes when God's will for me is to say no? Or vice versa? You see, although Jesus had a specific plan to establish a kingdom, the essence of the kingdom is the authority of the king. So my priority becomes submitting to Him in everything that I do."

"And living as He wants us to—that's His righteousness?" the young man asked.

---

*"One of the main keys is
to make God's will and God's
standards a guide for all
our decisions and activities."*

"Right. You see, quite a few of Jesus' listeners considered themselves specialists in righteousness. They knew all the laws of the Bible—the Ten Commandments and all the other Old Testament commands and prohibitions. Unfortunately, they didn't have the integrity of heart and life to please Him. When I think about His righteousness, I think of His standard. Let me show you what I mean."

Rising from his chair, the older man walked to the window. Inviting his companion to join him, he pointed to a construction project down the street. Numerous workmen were erecting a steel framework for a multistoried office building.

"How do you suppose they were able to get those pieces of steel to fit just right?"

"They measured them," the young man responded. "Used a ruler, a level—and they followed the blueprints."

"Precisely." Pointing to the Bible resting on his conference table, he said, "And right there is our plumb line, our level, our ruler. I think the verse we're talking about suggests that I make the Bible my standard for everything I say or do."

"That may be. But my impression is that a lot of Christians don't practice that. I've learned a lot lately about some pretty well-known preachers who seem to violate some of those standards."

"Unfortunately, you're right. And it's causing no end of anxiety and grief. Those unfortunate events just strengthen my contention that one of the main keys is to make God's will and God's standards a guide for all our decisions and activities."

"Interesting we should be discussing this. The other day, one of the men I work with at the office heard about this supposedly really great deal—sort of a tax shelter situation. Several of the guys in the office are getting into it. I thought about it myself. In fact, I had some funds I could have moved into the program, and I'd probably do pretty well. But I'm not sure how the program squares up with the tax laws."

The gray-haired man nodded. "I can understand the attractiveness of a proposition like that, especially if you can take advantage of it. I'm glad you were willing to consider the possibility that it might not measure up to God's standards."

"I'll probably give it some further thought—maybe talk with my tax attorney. I probably won't do it, though. But I still keep worrying about—thinking about—my wife. This cancer. I believe you said there's another key to worry-free living here somewhere."

"Check out the last verse in the chapter," replied the older man. "Verse 34. Read it, and see if you can figure out the key."

"'So don't be anxious about tomorrow. God will take care of your tomorrow too. Live one day at a time.' So He's saying, 'Don't worry about tomorrow.' But that's a big part of my problem. It's the uncertainty about tomorrow that's bugging me."

The older man stretched in his seat, raising both arms, then he turned to look directly at his friend. "I think you just hit on one of the most important components of anxiety. It's usually about the future, and the future is something over which we have almost no control."

"This sounds a lot like what you said about the first key. You know, that business about controlling what you can and leaving everything else up to God? It's almost like He's saying you have control over today but not the future."

A note of enthusiasm colored the voice of the older man as he replied, "That's a great insight! In fact, I think that's something I need to be reminded of quite often. I tend to worry about things that need to get done tomorrow, things beyond my control. I'm sure your wife's diagnosis is one of those things that would be hard for any of us not to worry about. But my memory card here has another version of Matthew 6:34. It says, 'Each day has enough trouble of its own' (NIV)."

He pulled a 3x5 card out of the stack, then held it over for the young man to examine. "Boy isn't that the truth!"

"We have enough trouble to take care of today. If we take care of today's trouble—like getting the medical care your wife needs, having the appropriate tests run, all that— and turn tomorrow's trouble over to God—I think that'll work. In fact, that's the principle we talked about the first time we got together—living one day at a time."

The young man smiled as he replied, "Life 101, eh?"

"But it works."

The young man nodded. "It sounds like it ought to, but I seem to be having a lot of trouble making it work. Got any suggestions?"

"What I have discovered is this: the more I pray, the less I worry."

"You figured I would, didn't you?" replied the older man as he flipped several pages in his Bible. "Remember the popular song of a few years back? 'Don't Worry, Be Happy'?"

"Yes. I thought it was sort of cute. But it's not part of the Bible, is it?"

"No, it's not. But there is a similar principle. Here in Philippians, chapter 4. Look at verse 6. If you paraphrased this verse into the title of a song—Paul's song—you might end up with 'Don't Worry, Be Prayerful.'"

The young man read the verse: "Don't worry about anything; instead, pray about everything; tell God your needs and don't forget to thank him for his answers."

"The next verse too. Go ahead."

"If you do this you will experience God's peace, which is far more wonderful than the human mind can understand."

The young man looked at his older friend. "You really believe this stuff, don't you? I've noticed from being around you that you don't seem like a worried man at all. You do a lot of praying?"

"Probably not as much as I should—but when do any of us really pray enough? After all, the Bible says to pray incessantly. You know, sort of like the way a person who has a bad cold or allergies keeps coughing over and over.

"What I have discovered is this: the more I pray, the less I worry. In fact, if I use anxiety as a signal to stop and pray—about anything, big or little—I find it makes a major difference. I think God cares about the big things—and even the little things. And I think if we discipline ourselves to pray about things, we'll be much less likely to be worried or uptight about them."

Now it was the young man's turn to lean back in his chair and stretch. "I guess I never thought about it that way. Now that you mention it, I can think of a lot of things I'd be less uptight about if I prayed about them—like how the boss may respond to a request for some time off to be with my wife if she needs to go into the hospital for surgery. Or whether Herman, the new guy in the office, will position himself to take over my spot if I take time off."

"There's one more thing to keep in mind," the young man's mentor added as he closed his Bible. "It didn't say God will always work things out the way you pray He will. What it did say was that the peace of God, which is beyond all understanding, will protect our hearts and minds."

"Could you explain that concept?"

"I'll give it a try. I think He's talking about peace of mind, which comes from God Himself, not from being able to figure out the situation. Paul was saying that, when we stop worrying and start praying about things, God will give us peace to protect us from emotional and mental turmoil.

"That's sure been my experience. I remember some years ago, my wife was giving birth to our oldest child. She lost a lot of blood. In fact, at one point, they weren't sure she'd make it. I'm not sure it would be accurate to say I was worried. 'Panic' would probably be a better word to describe my feelings. But I remembered this verse, and I prayed. It might have been the hardest praying I've ever done in my life. I was certainly relieved when the doctor came out to tell me she'd be OK. But, as I think back on it, I really began to feel peaceful about things when I started to pray about it. It really does work.

"There was a lady in a Bible study class I was involved in some years ago. Her name was Marie. She was very successful in business. Actually, you remind me of her in some ways. She was very sharp. But she used to be a world-champion worrier. I mean, every time you'd see or hear from her, she was worried about something. Then somebody shared these principles with her, and she became a world-champion prayer warrior. She organized all her prayer requests in a notebook and prayed about different things at different times. In fact, her system of prayer reminders was probably more effective than Day Timers, Executive Scan Cards, or any of those other time management systems. She's the kind of person I'd want praying for me if I were facing the kind of situation you and your wife are up against."

"Well, I'd sure like to enlist her prayers. What you've told me has helped a lot. I wasn't sure what to do. I just about couldn't function. Could you—would you pray for my wife?"

"Gladly," replied the One Minute Christian. "Why don't we, right now?"

10

LIGHTEN UP

The young man's face was bright red. Veins stood out in his neck like cords. Tension was reflected in his voice.

"I can't believe I did such a stupid thing—spilling coffee all over your notes, ruining your books! It's a disaster! I just can't stand myself when I do stupid things like this!"

A concerned look replaced the smile on the face of the man called the One Minute Christian. "And we were going to talk about having fun. Let me assure you that there's nothing in those notes that can't be replaced. Besides, my secretary is a specialist at disaster mop-up. In fact, it's such a beautiful day, why don't we get out of the office. Let's walk down to the park."

The young man quickly shook his head. "No, we can't do that. I need to clean this up. I'm the one who made the mess. I can't just go off and leave things like this."

Raising his right hand in the manner of a traffic officer, the older man said, "Now hold it. Hold it just a minute. Time out. I want you to understand something very important about what just happened."

Cringing, the young man looked up at his mentor. "Go ahead," he said, "lay it on me. I deserve it."

The older man surveyed the wreckage on his desk. Shattered pieces of cup spread across the carpet. "You drink your coffee with cream, don't you? Why?"

His voice tight with irritation, the young man replied, "What's that got to do with anything? I made just as big a mess with cream in the coffee as I would have if it were black."

Undaunted, the gray-haired man smiled. "Here's my point. You added creamer to lighten up the coffee. Maybe it's time to lighten up your attitude after this miniature disaster of sorts. Like I said, my secretary is a specialist in disaster containment. I think she could have handled things in Alaska better than those people they hired to clean up after that oil tanker."

Just then his secretary rushed in with towels in hand, prepared to attack the mess. The older man pulled several 3x5 cards off his desk, wiped them with one of the paper towels he grabbed from the secretary, and stuck them in his shirt pocket. Then he slipped a sweater from his hanger and said to his sharply dressed companion, "Follow me."

Reluctantly the young man obeyed.

Stepping into a crisp early-fall day awash in sunlight, the older man clipped a pair of sunglasses onto his spectacles. "Sometimes the best thing to do is to see a disaster through. But I've also discovered there's a time to leave things to others and get some distance. Some perspective."

The two men looked across the street at a group of elementary school children swarming across the playground. "See those kids?" he said to his companion. "They look like they don't have a care in the world. But for some of them, life is very difficult. Some of them have parents who could care less about whether they get the love and support they need. Others are regularly abused—emotionally, perhaps even physically or sexually. Just looking at them on the playground, you'd never know anything was wrong. But there's a lesson we can learn from that."

"What?" the young man asked through gritted teeth.

"It's a lesson that's hard for some of us to learn because we're perfectionists ourselves—hard-driving, responsible—and basically because we tend to be intense."

"I don't see what you're getting at. All I see is a group of school kids playing like they don't have a care in the world."

"That's exactly what I'm getting at. Some of them have just as many cares in the world as you or I. In fact, some of them had things happen to them this very morning that are far worse than your little disaster. I mean, abusing a child's body or mind is a lot worse than spilling coffee on a few papers. And it's not as if those notes on my desk were the Magna Charta or the Declaration of Independence. So lighten up, OK?"

Struggling with his emotions, the young man said, "OK, I'll try. So what are we going to do?"

"For a start, let's walk down to that little park on the corner and grab a bench. Then we'll talk about having fun."

As the One Minute Christian strode purposefully down the steps, his companion walked along beside him, fuming. *First, I get stuck in a horrible traffic jam. Then I pour coffee all over his office. And now he's talking about having fun. Sometimes he's unreal.*

The older man whistled as the two men strolled along the leaf-strewn sidewalk. A brisk northerly wind was moderated by the warmth of the sun. The wind carried the sounds of the children at play, along with the distant smell of burning leaves. The two men reached the little park at the corner and took seats on a bench facing the school and playground. For a time, neither spoke.

"There's a difference between getting serious about God and letting your life be overrun with seriousness."

Finally the young man broke the silence. "I just don't get it. I come into your office, take up your time, spill coffee on your notes, practically ruin your day, and here we are sitting in a park. And you're whistling. Don't you ever get angry?"

"Sure. I get angry more often than I ever did before. For the first ten years of my marriage, I was never angry at my wife."

The surprised look on the face of the young man was reflected in his voice, "You've gotta be kidding! How could you be married for that long and never get upset about any-thing?"

"That's my point. It wasn't that I never became angry. You could ask my wife; she'd tell you. And she could tell when I was angry. I was just into a lot of denial about what I was really upset about. In those days I was probably more intense than you are. If something interrupted my schedule, like a traffic jam—I think I did hear you mention a traffic jam when you arrived—it really disturbed me. And if I did some-thing wrong, I was on my own case like flies on honey. I guess I've learned a thing or two about anger over the years. It's helped me lighten up. At least life is more fun now."

"I don't get it. Having fun isn't one of my major con-cerns in life right now. After all, I've decided to get serious about spiritual things."

"Maybe there's a difference between getting serious about God and letting your life be overrun with seriousness. I think it was Solomon who said there's a time and purpose for everything under heaven. A time to laugh, a time to cry, a time to be born, a time to die, a time to love, a time to hate—and I guess it would be OK to say a time to have fun.

"You see, some people teach that anything that's fun must be either unhealthy, immoral, or unspiritual. But I see a lot of fun in the Bible—and even a lot of humor. It's a matter of finding the right place and time for everything."

The young man shifted positions on the bench, crossed his leg, and faced his mentor. The gray-haired man contin-ued. "There were several times in the Bible when Jesus be-came angry. Once was when a group of Pharisees attempted to put to death a woman taken in adultery. They said they caught her in the very act. So they were all set to stone her. He let them know how He felt about that by suggesting that whoever was without sin should cast the first stone."

"That's pretty strong," the young man responded. "I can relate to that, though. A few weeks ago I felt like stoning my wife—not to mention the guy she was involved with. But

I guess the men Jesus was talking to didn't stone that woman after all, did they?"

"Nope. There was another time when He was teaching in a synagogue. A man there had a paralyzed hand, and the Pharisees were watching Jesus so they could charge him with a crime if He healed this man on the Sabbath. You see, that was against their law. Jesus looked around at them with anger—He was grieved because of the hardness of their hearts. Then He went ahead and restored the man's paralyzed hand so that it was as sound as the other one."

The young man ran his fingers through his hair. "I remember your telling me about Jesus getting angry. I had always believed it was a sin to get angry—no matter what the situation."

The older man chuckled, then turned in his seat so that he was facing his younger companion. "I think I had that drilled into me from the time I was very young. You know, anger is always wrong. You should never get mad or angry. No matter what, anger is always a sin. The trouble is, I was angry a lot of the time. Both my beliefs and my practice were out of step with Scripture."

"I think I'm angry quite a bit of the time too. My wife has been on me about getting upset so often, especially over little things. She thinks I really need to do something about it."

"The problem is that sometimes we have five dollars' worth of anger over a fifty-cent event."

Nodding in understanding, the older man replied, "Sometimes what we need to do is just understand what anger is all about. Then it's easier to learn how to be angry when we need to be angry, and lighten up when we need to lighten up. Remember recently when that guy drove a pickup truck through the window of a cafeteria in Central Texas?

Jumped out of his car and started shooting people? He killed more people than any other mass murderer at one time. Even more than Charles Manson or Richard Speck. But I wasn't as angry about that as I was about the fact that I knew one of those people personally. He killed one of my friends."

For a moment there was a catch in the gray-haired man's voice. He paused as he regained his composure. "It's still hard for me to think of the fact that my friend is gone. And it was so senseless. A lot of the things Jesus was angry about were things like that—when people wanted to hurt other people or do something that was contrary to God's nature."

"You mean like keep a crippled man from being healed? That seems pretty bad."

"I think that's the thing about anger." The older man paused, shook his head, and removed his glasses. Then he began to polish them. "I think it's OK to be angry about the terrible things that happen to others. In fact, I've learned the hard way that it's even OK to be angry about the bad things that happen to *us.* The problem is that sometimes we have five dollars' worth of anger over a fifty-cent event."

A glimmer of understanding touched the young man's face. "You mean, like blowing a whole day over one spilled cup of coffee?"

"Something like that. There's something else about anger that's important to remember. It's sort of like a school-zone warning light."

The young man followed the direction of his older companion's extended index finger. He noticed two amber flashing lights bracketing a sign that said, "Warning. School Zone." Cars slowed noticeably as they drove past.

"You see, anger is like that warning sign. It's not good or bad in itself. But it can warn us about the possibility of something bad, some danger to ourselves or to others. The key is how we handle our anger. When we notice the light going off, what do we do? Some people stuff their anger away—you know, sort of like ignoring the light. Pretending it's not there. That's certainly not healthy. But neither is it healthy to always blow people away with our anger.

"What I've discovered is that, first of all, it's important for me to look at what's causing the anger—especially if there's some other underlying emotion. Like grief or loneliness or envy. Or fear. A lot of times fear is the underlying emotion. Or maybe it's just perfectionism out of control. Sometimes, when we feel like things are out of control, our anger just boils to the surface, and the results are devastating."

"I think I've been living pretty close to the boiling point lately," the young man admitted. "I'm still not sure I understand completely why. I've been afraid I'd do something really disastrous—you know, at work or at home."

"I know what you mean. One of my heroes in the Bible is Peter. He was pretty upset when they came to arrest Jesus. In fact, I think he was afraid he would deny the Lord. I'm pretty sure he felt that way because, just before this all happened, he told Jesus, 'I'll never forsake you Lord, even if everybody else does.' And just a few hours later, he denied that he even knew Him.

"Anyway, when the priests and the soldiers came to arrest Jesus, Peter pulled out a sword and cut off a man's ear. Jesus not only told him to put up his sword, but He healed the man's ear. The point is, Peter had to have been really angry to have pulled that sword in the first place."

"He must have been a pretty good swordsman to whack off a guy's ear."

"I don't think so. In my opinion, Peter was a lousy swordsman. I think he was aiming for the man's head. It was what I guess you could call a 'providential miss.' Anyway, what I've learned to do when I'm angry is try to figure out what I'm really upset about. *What's* really bothering me? Is it what's happening now? Or is it something that's happened before that's still unresolved.

"Then I ask, *Who* am I angry at? Am I angry at someone else? Am I angry over a circumstance? Am I angry at a person? Maybe myself? Perhaps I'm even angry at God! The main thing is, I need to be honest about my anger. Then I need to see if there is an underlying emotion I haven't faced.

"For example, my wife used to really get upset with me when I didn't get home when I promised her I would. I never took those deadlines very seriously. I mean, after all, I was busy doing important things. It took me a while to realize that being home for dinner with her and the kids was important too.

"But as we learned to communicate with each other, what I discovered was that not only did she have a legitimate reason to be angry, underneath that anger she was lonely. She really just wanted to be with me.

"Then there were times when people asked me to do things, and I'd get angry with them—you know, things I didn't feel like I *could* do. It turned out my anger was a way to mask my fear of failure."

The older man paused, then looked over at the school playground where several teachers were herding the children into a straight line. A number of stragglers were attempting to squeeze a few more seconds out of their play period.

"Is all this making any sense?" the older man asked.

"I think so. I mean, I think I'm getting the picture that it's OK to be angry at times, but it's got to be for the right reason."

"That's a good way to put it. Then we have to decide how to handle it. The apostle Paul must have been a pretty angry man when he was a Pharisee. At least that's the picture we get when he was throwing Christians in jail right and left. Later on, after he had been in ministry for several years, he gave the Ephesian Christians some suggestions about what to do with their anger. That's when he told them to become angry but not to sin. Not to let the sun go down on their anger."

The young man interrupted, "I remember your telling me about that. Anger and bitterness. You said that, if we allowed anger to build up in our lives without dealing with it, it was like storing up garbage. But I still don't see the harm in letting it go for a while. I mean, after all, we collect garbage in plastic bags today. Then the collection truck comes by once a week to pick up the bags of garbage."

"That's where the analogy breaks down. There isn't a garbage truck to collect our anger. We have to personally choose to forgive. Whenever we become aware of feelings of anger, if we don't get in touch with those feelings, understand where they're coming from, we just repress them—push them back out of sight.

"Let me tell you about something that happened to me not too long ago. My wife and I were having company—a married couple we'd been looking forward to visiting with for a long time. We were both late getting home, and the house was a mess. I collected a bag of garbage and stuffed it in the kitchen pantry behind a big box of cat litter. We cleaned up the rest of the house, had a great evening with our friends, and things were fine for a few days. But I suspect you can guess what eventually happened."

"I guess it got pretty smelly."

"Phew, it sure was," replied his mentor. "And that's how our lives get when we let unresolved anger build up in them. It's also unhealthy."

"A person who's happy on the inside will tend to be more healthy than the individual who's constantly in a negative, depressed, or angry frame of mind."

Pulling out the 3x5 cards from his pocket that he had picked up earlier, he looked at them, then handed one to his young companion. "Take a look at this."

The young man read. "A cheerful heart does good like medicine, but a broken spirit makes one sick" (Proverbs 17:22).

"That's one of three statements about a cheerful or joyful heart in Proverbs. You know, Solomon was one of the wisest people who ever lived. I have found his proverbs helpful to me in a lot of areas—in business, in dealing with people, you name it.

"But I think those statements about a cheerful heart have been as helpful as anything I've read. They really taught me to lighten up. That's why I have them on these cards—so I can pull them out and look at them when I need reminding."

"You need reminding?" The young man looked puzzled.

"Sure. Just yesterday I was playing phone tag with a man I needed to talk with. I was about to drive my secretary to distraction, not to mention myself. Plus I was wasting a lot of time—and some emotional energy I couldn't spare.

"Finally, I remembered these cards. Took a look at them and decided to quit calling every quarter hour. About half an hour later, just as I was putting together the report I needed to talk with him about, he called!

"I think Solomon's point is well taken. Medical studies bear it out. A person who's happy on the inside will tend to be more healthy than the individual who's constantly in a negative, depressed, or angry frame of mind.

"Now, there is a time for us to grieve losses, but I think it's important that our spirit not remain crushed or grieved. Otherwise, we'll be like an older person who's chronically sick and whose bones are brittle and dried up—even if we're not that old physically."

"I think I see what you're getting at," the young man responded. "One of the vice presidents at work has sort of been known as the hatchet man because he likes to fire people. Seems he's always angry or upset about something. About six weeks ago he had a heart attack—just dropped in his tracks. Most of the people at the office simply think he had it coming."

"There may have been other factors," the One Minute Christian added, "but I've read studies that indicate that the angry Type A person is more prone to heart attacks and other health problems than other types."

"You're hitting pretty close to home now. Bringing up that Type A business. I'm sure you recall that I'm pretty much a Type A."

With a twinkle in his eyes, the older man responded, "But so am I."

Handing the young man a second card, he said, "Look this over."

The young man read, "A happy heart makes the face cheerful, but heartache crushes the spirit" (Proverbs 15:13, NIV).

"Have you ever noticed," the older man asked, "how just being around some people can lift your spirits? I mean, just seeing the smile radiating from their face. Then there are some people who are just like a breath of foul air. They seem to discourage themselves and everybody else in their wake.

"I've noticed that you have the capacity to be one of those cheerful individuals who can have that kind of positive impact on other people. But you need to be able to handle those bouts of anger when they come up."

"Let me see the other card," the young man said. Taking it from the older man, he held it up to the sunlight and read, "'All the days of the oppressed are wretched, but the cheerful heart has a continual feast' (Proverbs 15:15). What a great verse!"

"You know, bad things happen to all of us," the One Minute Christian pointed out. "Broken coffee cups, traffic tickets, bouts with the flu, misunderstandings at work. Even serious things like mental crises, threats of cancer. Nobody's cup is completely full of good things. But then again, nobody's is completely empty. Take that cup of coffee you spilled."

"I'd like to take it back, but I guess it's too late for that."

"But let's think about it for a minute. You had already taken several sips from it, as I recall. Was it half-full, or was it half-empty?"

"Half-emp—I really don't know," the young man responded. "I guess either answer would be correct. It's just how you look at it."

"So take another look at that card. Tell me what you think it says.

"It looks like some people are always gloomy. They seem to feel like they're afflicted or persecuted—they see every day as a bad day. Other people have a cheerful outlook on life. They must feel pretty good about things."

"Very good!" the older man responded, obvious enthusiasm in his voice. "You catch on quickly. But it's one thing to catch on while we're sitting out here on a park bench watching carefree people chase each other around a tree or school kids race around a playground. It's another thing when we're caught in a traffic jam or someone insults us, lies about us, or cheats on us."

"Or when we spill coffee all over someone else's desk," the young man grinned. "Maybe I really do need to lighten up."

With a smile on his face also, the gray-haired man rose to his feet. "Is that lighten up with Half & Half or powdered creamer?"

11

DON'T DESPISE
LITTLE THINGS

About two more minutes and I'm going to get really hacked," the young man said to himself. He had to be talking to himself since no one else was in the car. "This is why I hate to come downtown. It's always a traffic jam, and there's never a parking place. Why can't there ever be a parking place? Why do people always pull out of their parking places just after I pass?"

It was getting hard for the young man to maintain a cheerful heart as the man he often called the One Minute Christian had encouraged him to do. He was too keenly aware that if this aggravating parking problem dragged on for much longer he would be terribly late. The older man was probably already waiting for him at the restaurant on the top floor of a nearby skyscraper.

The previous afternoon, near the close of business, his secretary had handed him a message from his mentor. When he returned the call, the older man explained that a conflict had come up—a meeting he had to attend downtown. He suggested that they reschedule their planned meeting and meet for lunch downtown. "There's a neat restaurant at the top of Park Towers—you know, the building that's lighted so brilliantly at night—the one that's sort of become a landmark for the city."

"How can I miss it?" the young man replied. "But I've

never eaten there. Hard to believe, isn't it. What time will your meeting be over?"

"Let's meet at quarter-till-twelve. That way we'll miss a little bit of the lunch rush. Maybe we can get a table next to the window."

The young professional glanced at the expensive watch on his wrist for the fifth time in the last two minutes. "Eleven minutes to twelve," he muttered. "This wouldn't be so bad if I were there right now. But by the time I get parked, the restaurant will be packed."

Finally, spotting a parking garage a block away, the young man risked his expensive imported automobile and cut across two lanes of traffic. Tires screeched as he wheeled into the lot, slammed on the brakes, threw open the door, and handed the keys to the attendant. Be careful with it," he yelled over his shoulder as he dashed out of the parking lot and down the street toward Park Tower.

Racing across the intersection that separated him from the glass-covered skyscraper just as the light was changing, he rushed toward the building lobby. It seemed packed.

Just what I need. Something's going on down here— an art show of all things!

Trying not to be too disruptive, the young man pushed his way through the crowds of people who filled the lobby of the building. Noticing an elevator open in front of him, he rushed over. Just as he was about to enter, he glanced up. The sign above the car read, "This elevator does not go to the restaurant."

Relieved that he hadn't gotten on, but gritting his teeth, the young man turned to survey the bank of elevators. Finally he spotted one with a sign reading, "Restaurant." Elbowing his way through the crowd and twice apologizing for jostling others, he eventually found himself standing in front of the elevator doors.

What's holding things up now? he wondered.

After what seemed like at least two eternities, the car finally arrived. When it had emptied, he rushed into the compartment and rode to the top floor. Quickly stepping off the elevator, the young man immediately noticed several upset people talking with the maître d'. But his friend was nowhere to be seen. Just as he was about to join the harried line, the young man glanced over at a corner of the waiting area. There, sitting in a chair, shielded from the crowd by a large, planted shrub, sat his friend, quietly reading a book.

When the young man cleared his throat, the older man looked up. "Ah, a familiar voice. Looks like you made it OK."

"I'm not sure I'd go that far. I think I was being tested on the subject of our discussion last week."

"You mean the crowds and the traffic? It's always a zoo downtown, isn't it?"

"You can say that again. I've been looking for a parking place for the last fifteen minutes. And an art show in the lobby, of all things. I wonder if—"

He was interrupted by the maître d', who walked directly from his post to the young man's mentor. Calling him by name, he said, "Your table is ready."

The young man could hardly conceal his surprise. "How did *that* happen?" he asked as soon as the two men were seated—at a choice window table. "I'm impressed! You must really be connected with these people."

"I've been here a time or two. But the main thing is that I got to be friends with the maître d' when he was working in a small restaurant near my office. I used to go in there at least once a week, and we spent quite a bit of time talking. So now, if I have to be downtown here—which happens occasionally—I give him a call. He seems to get a kick out of making me and the people with me feel special."

"I've eaten at a lot of fancy restaurants in a lot of cities. But I don't think I've ever been treated any better. And you say all you did was call him and ask?"

"That's right. But I used to be reluctant to do that. When I first found out he was working here, he told me to call him whenever I was coming. I didn't. And the next time I was here, he spotted me. Got on my case. Asked me why I didn't call him to make a reservation. I told him I didn't want to bother him.

"He told me it was no bother. That he really wanted to take care of people who were his friends. He said he felt like that's one reason God gave him a job at such a posh restaurant."

"Why would I want to bother God about something as trivial as lost papers? That would be like wasting my boss's time asking where the paper clips were."

The two men noticed their server standing quietly nearby, paused in their conversation to accept menus, then looked them over. Both men made their selections without delay. The young server brought water and iced tea. As the older man squeezed lemon into his tea, he asked his friend, "By the way, I didn't get a chance to ask you last week. How's your prayer life going?"

"Well, I've been doing a lot more praying and less worrying, I think. I've still been concerned about my wife's physical condition. I prayed a lot about that—and our finances too. And with all the things going on in Russia, I've been praying a lot about that. But I didn't pray at all yesterday. At least I don't remember praying. I lost some papers I needed to have for a meeting. Just about drove me up a wall before I finally found 'em filed in another client's folder. Losing those papers really knocked my prayer life for a loop."

Placing his napkin in his lap, the gray-haired man paused, then asked, "Did you think about praying for God to help you find those papers?"

"You've got to be kidding," the young man replied, catching his voice before he raised it over the muted sound of nearby diners. "Why would I want to bother God about something as trivial as lost papers? That would be like wasting my boss's time asking where the paper clips were."

"Maybe that's part of the problem. Perhaps you're viewing God as if He were like your boss. If your boss is like a lot of people's bosses—and some of the bosses I've had—he wouldn't want to be bothered about little things. But there *are* bosses who really do care about those little things and who are glad to be asked about them. Remind me to tell you a story about the CEO of one of the largest companies of its kind in the country—a man who used to be my immediate boss. He was incredibly thoughtful about little things.

"But before I do that, I want to tell you where I got the idea about praying about lost papers. I suspect from the look on your face that you were wondering whether my elevator went all the way to the top floor when I suggested that. Or maybe you thought I was a few bricks shy of a load."

Noticing the twinkle in his friend's eye, the young man smiled himself. "Well—I wasn't sure quite where you were coming from. Where did you get that idea about praying for missing papers. There's not anything in the Bible about it, is there? I mean, did Moses or Abraham ever pray about lost papers? Or did Paul lose one of the letters he wrote for the New Testament?"

The older man chuckled. "Probably not. And I doubt if Jesus ever wrote anything on paper—much less lost it.

"Actually I learned this lesson about praying about missing things from my mother."

"Your mother?" the young man exclaimed. "That was a long time ago!"

The older man smiled. "I grew up about twenty miles or so outside the city—it was a good deal smaller than this, but it was still pretty big. Back then they didn't have shopping centers—we did most of our shopping downtown. Mother didn't have a driver's license, and Dad worked most of the time—so we rode the bus. When I turned sixteen, I had my driver's license in about twenty-four hours, and you can probably guess the first thing I wanted to do."

"Drive to town?"

"Not much mystery there. Just as we were ready to go, we realized the keys to the car were missing. We looked for half an hour—it seemed a lot longer, though. Turned the house upside down. But no car keys. Finally, Mother—bless her heart, I thought she was crazy—suggested we pray about it. I told her how I felt. She looked at me in that way of hers and said, 'Son, don't ever think anything is too big to take to God in prayer. And don't ever think anything is too little, either.' She bowed her head right there and asked God to help us find those keys."

"Flight connections? You pray about flight connections?"

"So you found the keys immediately?"

"Not hardly," the older man chuckled. "It was about ten minutes later. I found them in my room. Guess I'd picked 'em up without thinking and left them in my room, knowing I was about to drive to town for the first time."

"Sounds like that made a pretty strong impression on you. Didn't you ever try praying for something and not find it?"

"Sure," smiled his mentor. "That's happened to me before, but not as often as you think. More frequently, the Lord's been pleased to help me with whatever I'd lost."

"What about the times when He didn't?"

"At first I couldn't figure out what God was trying to do. But finally I understood. He was just trying to teach me patience. That, and appreciation for the times when He did help me—like with flight connections."

"Flight connections? You pray about flight connections?" The young man's face showed his surprise.

"Back when I used to travel more, I often found myself running through airports, sort of like O. J. Simpson on that old rental car commercial, trying to make a flight connection. At first I'd really get upset about the tight connection, the delays—especially if I missed a flight. Then I remembered the lesson I learned as a kid—about praying about little things. So I started praying about my connections."

"Did that help you make your flights?"

"Sometimes. In fact, quite often, I believe. Most of all, it helped my attitude about things." The older man grinned. "It's sort of hard to gripe and pray about something at the same time."

"I guess that's something I should add to my list of things to pray about—especially since I fly so much."

Reaching into the pocket of his muted plaid sport coat, the older man removed a card, looked at it for a moment, then handed it to his companion. Just then the waiter appeared with their lunch portions. "Look that over while we concentrate of this good food for a while."

At the older man's suggestion, the two men paused to express thanks for their food, then spent several minutes enjoying the meal and commenting on the view. "Check out those clouds," the older man noted, pointing out the window toward the west. "I was in here a few months ago during a summer thunderstorm. We were right in the middle of it—lightening all around. It was the most incredible thing. My wife was with me—she was rather frightened by the whole thing. Not that I wasn't a bit concerned myself, you understand."

"So did you pray about it?"

"Now that you mention it, we did. I'm not sure at the time we would have considered that praying about a small thing. Although as storms go, it wasn't too big or intense. My biggest concern was being hit by lightning—we were sitting near the window. I also found myself wondering if the storm had spawned a tornado. No telling what that might have done to this building."

Picking up the 3x5 card from the white linen tablecloth, the young man stared at the words. "For who has despised the day of small things? (Zechariah 4:10, NKJV)."

"Where do you find all these verses? I'm not sure I even knew there was a book of Zechariah."

"It's in the Old Testament, in a section called the Minor Prophets. Although they weren't really minor—it's just that they wrote shorter books than the ones we typically call the Major Prophets—Isaiah, Jeremiah, and Ezekiel."

"I think I see the connection with missing keys or papers. Or even flight connections. Basically, they're small things, right?"

"Right."

The young man rubbed the back of his neck, then shifted the position of his chair. "But what does this have to do with what you've been telling me? I guess what I'm saying is that the picture's still a little fuzzy."

Settling back into his chair, the older man paused reflectively and took a sip of his iced tea. "For a long time after I became a Christian, I believed God answered prayer. But I mainly prayed about—you know—major things. Like the salvation of my lost relatives, miraculous cures for people with cancer. I was sort of aware of what my mother had taught me about praying for small things. In fact, sometimes I did pray about little things. But it never really clicked.

"Then one day I was reading through these so-called Minor Prophets. Right in the middle of Zechariah I came across this little verse. 'Who has despised the day of small things?' It was like God took that statement out of Scripture, hit me over the head with it, and made it all click. Don't discount little things.

"At the time I had been teaching a Bible study—a small group of people in a community about an hour's drive from where we were living. Several of the couples in the group were quite a bit older than I was. But one couple was about the same age as my wife and I. They were the people I was really excited about. I sort of considered them the key people to whom I was ministering. And wouldn't you know it, that very week the man's company transferred him to another city. They moved immediately—in fact, we haven't seen them since.

"When they were transferred, I told my wife I was just about ready to give up what I was doing. After all, it was a very small group of people, and we just lost the people I considered to be the best prospects."

The One Minute Christian paused and took another sip from his iced tea. "That was the very week I discovered that verse. I'm sure I'd read it before, but I had never seen it like I saw it then."

"So you continued to teach those people? I can certainly see where you could have considered it a waste of your time—you know, maybe found something more productive, perhaps even something bigger."

"I guess that's what was in the back of my mind. But then I thought about that verse. Zechariah—kind of an obscure character—was the one who made that statement. Made it to a man named Zerubbabal—he was even more obscure."

The young man's puzzled look turned to a grin as his older companion chuckled. "You've never heard of either of them, have you?"

"Can't say as I have. But, then, there are a lot of people in the Bible I've probably never heard of."

"Don't hesitate to take those little things to God—even those things you consider beneath His time or trouble."

"This guy Zerubbabal was rebuilding the Temple. Only it was about a tenth of the size and glamour of the original Temple Solomon built."

"What happened to the original? Catch fire and burn down?"

"No. It was destroyed by the Babylonians when they captured Jerusalem. Sort of like what the Iraqis would like to do today. When the Israelites came back after seventy years in captivity, they built this plain little Temple—sort of the difference between a top-of-the-line BMW and an old Volkswagen Beetle."

The young man chuckled again, thinking about his sleek BMW 735i. "I get the picture. So they figured that was quite a comedown."

THE ONE MINUTE CHRISTIAN

"No doubt about it. That's when Zechariah told them not to despise the day of small things."

"Despise—so they really hated that little Temple?"

"Not actually. The word *despise* may be a little misleading. It can mean to hate something—or it can mean just to treat something as unimportant or kind of lightweight. You know, not take it seriously. That was what they were doing with their Temple. I think God wanted them to know —and us too—that little things can be important."

At this point the waiter paused at their table. "Dessert anyone?"

"Not for me," the gray-haired man said. "But I will take a cup of that dark-roast coffee you're famous for. Try it," he suggested to his friend. "It's just a little cup, but it sure is good."

The young man nodded. The waiter went to get their coffee, and the older man resumed his conversation. Turning over the card with the verse written on it, he removed a pen from his pocket. "Let me jot down three little things related to this little statement—little reminders of ways you can make this principle a part of your life."

He quickly scrawled a sentence on the paper, then turned it around so his friend could see, "In case you can't read my writing that says, 'Principle #1: Trust God for little things.' What I mean is, don't hesitate to take those little things to God—even those things you consider beneath His time or trouble. There's a statement in Matthew 6, the verses we discussed a couple weeks ago—that talks about the hairs on your head."

"You mean the verse that says even the hairs on your head are numbered?"

"Right. And if God is concerned about the hair I've been losing—and I seem to be losing a lot of hair lately; some of it winds up on my comb every time I comb it—I'm sure he's concerned about other little things.

"Let me tell you about a missionary I met several years ago. He grew up as a boy on a mission field in India— wound up going back there. He's with the Lord now, but I heard him tell us all these neat little things God did for him. I used to think it was some kind of a joke. Then one year at a missions conference at our church we sat next to each other at a missionary luncheon. I found out this guy was for real! He actually did pray about things like his old car breaking down—he drove a sedan built shortly after World War II— getting over physical problems like a sore throat in time to preach, meeting people he wanted to witness to. This was sort of phase three in my introduction to little things. I still had a tendency to think of them as—well—little things. This guy convinced me those things I considered to be small are really important to God. Ever since then I've been operating on that premise. It's made quite a difference in my life."

Funny I've never heard anybody preach about that, the young man thought. Out loud he said, "It seems to me that God would be more concerned that we do great things for Him. I mean, doesn't the Bible say that, or something like it?"

"Not exactly. I do remember, when I was a teenager, hearing a camp speaker challenge us to expect great things from God and attempt great things for God. But I don't think that takes anything away from God's concern about the little things in my life."

Taking back the card, the older man added a second line to what he had written before, then showed it to his companion.

"Principle #2: Pay attention to little things."

"Now this may seem contradictory to what we talked about last week—you know, not having a five dollar reaction to a fifty cent irritant. But there are some little things we do need to pay close attention to. For example, I know you have an expensive automobile. I'd hate to even guess how much it costs."

He probably doesn't have a clue, the young man thought. *It probably cost as much as he makes in a year.*

"Do you use the cheapest brand of oil in your car?"

The young man shook his head vigorously. "Not a chance. I have it changed regularly. Use only the best grade of oil on the market."

"That's a great example of the importance of certain little things. I suspected you took care of your car that way. When I first learned to drive, one of the earliest lessons my dad taught me was the importance of changing the oil regularly—and checking it frequently.

"Then there was a man I worked with several years ago. He was an accountant, an older man who had started off as a carpenter on a construction crew. He took his accounting very seriously—had a sign on his desk that said, 'He who doesn't honor the penny isn't worth the dollar.' He really practiced that motto too."

"Sounds like some of the bean-counters in our office," said the young man. "Especially since the threat of that corporate takeover. Those guys have really cut down on expense accounts, travel, even marketing. They're watching everything, it seems."

"Don't discount the potentially big impact of little things."

"There's a lesson to be learned in that. Christian living isn't a matter of legalistically watching things—but we do need to be careful about little areas of inconsistency in our lives. Solomon suggested that it was the little foxes that usually spoiled the grapevines. To be honest with you, sometimes I find it harder to resist a little temptation to be irritated over something or to not take someone else's concerns seriously than I do some big temptation like embezzling a large sum of money or trying to seduce someone else's wife. I think the one who tempts us knows that if he can get us on several little things, it can lead to big things."

"Maybe that's what happened to my wife—you know, why she got involved. Probably a series of little things, some of which were my fault. But you know, what you've been telling me about forgiveness has really helped. I'm taking things a day at a time. Even the little things are getting better at home now."

The older man picked up his glass of water and took a long swallow. "One more thing, then I guess I'd better get going."

He wrote a final line on the back of the card. The young man read it: "Principle #3: Don't discount the potentially big impact of little things."

"Remember that tree in the park down the street from my office—the one we sat next to on the bench last week?"

"Yeah. It's an oak isn't it?"

"Last time I checked. Now, I'm not that knowledgeable about trees, but I'm pretty sure it's an oak—partially because of the acorns those squirrels were chasing. It's hard to imagine something that big, that grand, coming from a little seed about this size," he said, putting together thumb and forefinger to show the approximate size of an acorn. "I promised you a story at the beginning of the meal, and I'll tell it now, but I'll make it brief.

"Some time ago, I had scheduled a meeting with the man I mentioned to you earlier—Frank, the CEO of an important company. He was in town on business, and I was supposed to meet with him at noon for lunch at his hotel. Unfortunately, it was one of those days when everything fell apart. Twice I had to call him to apologize for running late. Finally, by about three o'clock, my staff and I put out most of the brushfires at my office. It took me half-an-hour through traffic to get to his hotel. Since it was so late, we had already decided not to meet in the restaurant. He told me to come on up to his room.

"When I arrived, room service was just leaving. The roast beef sandwich they had brought in smelled so good I was tempted to forget my manners and rush over to take a bite out of it. Of course, I didn't let myself do that. I shook hands, introduced myself—this was the first time we had met in person—and suggested he go ahead and eat. I didn't say anything about not having eaten myself, although I sure wanted to.

"Was I ever surprised when Frank said, 'That sandwich is for you. I figured you hadn't had a chance to eat, based on what you told me about your day. I went ahead and ordered a little while ago—I'm diabetic, so I had to eat. But I took the liberty to order for you. Hope you like roast beef.'

"That little act of friendship left a lasting, indelible mark on me. A couple years later, Frank offered me a position in his company. We worked together closely for several years—and he's still one of my best friends. And I'm convinced that our friendship, from a human perspective, grew out of that one little act of thoughtfulness.

"Now, we may have eventually become friends anyway, even if he'd ordered a sandwich and eaten it in front of me without offering me any. But that's not the kind of person he was."

"I think I'm getting your point," the young man said. "Little things really can make a big difference—whether we're praying about them or practicing them."

Reaching in his wallet to retrieve a gold credit card, he handed it quickly to the waiter after glancing at the check. Then he continued, "I've always considered myself a 'big picture' person. If it wasn't big enough or important enough, I just ignored it. You've given me more than just a good meal and a beautiful setting. You've given me some more food for thought. I think I'll start looking for little things. See if I can't notice all the little ways God may be doing things in my life."

The waiter returned and handed the young man his check. He signed it, removed his copy with practiced ease, quickly handed the other copies to the waiter, then pocketed his credit card. As the two men stood up to leave, his mentor asked, "By the way, can we switch our meeting next week to Tuesday morning?"

"Oh!" the young man exclaimed, slapping his forehead. "That would be fine. I almost forgot—my wife has a doctor's appointment on Monday, and I want to take off from work to go with her. That's gonna work out fine. I guess I'll consider that the first 'little thing' on my list."

12

NEVER GIVE UP

The man sometimes referred to as the One Minute Christian was raking leaves in his backyard when the phone rang. He had been thinking about how pleasantly warm and comfortable the weather was—especially since the series of cool, rainy days the previous week had hindered him from getting to his chores, such as raking leaves and repairing a screen on a first floor window.

"I think it's that young man you've been meeting with —he sounds pretty upset," his wife said as she handed him the cordless telephone.

The older man was greeted by the familiar voice. But it was obvious from the first few words that something was wrong. "Could I see you first thing Monday morning? Something's come up—I don't think it can wait until Tuesday."

"Sounds like something pretty serious." He gave his wife a knowing look. She quickly nodded and smiled. Taking that as his cue he said, "Would you like to come on over this afternoon? The wife and I try to make it a point not to plan anything for Saturday afternoons. I'm just raking a few leaves—I'm sure they can wait. In fact, why don't you bring your wife with you? It's time we got our wives together, especially since we've been meeting now for some time. Maybe we can visit a bit, then go grab a bite to eat."

After giving directions to his friend, the older man hung up the phone, chatted briefly with his wife, then resumed his yard work. About an hour later, as the older man was bagging the last of the leaves from his front yard, a platinum BMW turned the corner and pulled up in front of his house.

The young man was dressed in designer jeans, western boots, and an orange plaid shirt. After greeting his friend he introduced his wife. She was tall—almost as tall as her husband. Her naturally-wavy blonde hair was fashionably pulled back, and she wore a lavender sweater and white designer slacks. It was obvious to the older man that his young friend was extremely upset, while his wife seemed relatively calm.

"Let's head inside. The wife has fixed a pot of coffee— and hot herbal tea. I know the weather's a bit warm, but I always enjoy the selection of herbal teas she keeps on hand."

Inside the older man introduced his wife—a petite, energetic lady with sparkling brown eyes, a cheerful voice, and just a few streaks of gray in her dark brown hair.

"I'm so glad you both could come by," she greeted their visitors. "In a few minutes we'll have chocolate chip cookies." She smiled at her husband good-naturedly. "They're his favorite—even though he eats too many of them. He's told me about meeting with you." She turned her smile toward the young man. "I'm so glad the two of you could come over. I'll go see to the cookies."

"Let me join you," the young woman suggested. The two ladies headed to the kitchen while the older man invited his friend into his combination office/den. A green plaid couch and a brown corduroy recliner occupied one corner. Two whole sides of the room were taken up with built-in bookcases.

The young man walked over to look at the titles—history, theology, counseling—even fiction. "I see you like Robert Parker," he commented.

"I haven't found very many novelists who can turn a phrase the way he does—or who seem to have as much insight into the way people think. I don't always agree with his approach to some issues—but I respect his writing ability."

The older man pulled down the cover on a large antique roll-top desk in still another corner of the room. "No use our having to look at this clutter—I was just doing some studying this morning." Then he invited his guest to a place on the couch.

Before the older man could speak again, the young man blurted out, "You sure can't tell it from looking at her—but the tests confirmed that my wife has cancer." His voice broke as he tried to continue. "We—we found out when they called yesterday. When I found out that they phoned to see if we could come in later that day instead of waiting until Monday, I figured something was wrong."

The young man sat on the couch, fighting to regain his composure. A couple of tears slipped from the corner of his eye. One fell directly onto the crystal of his watch. The older man waited without speaking.

Finally, his young friend was able to speak again. "I—I didn't expect this to happen. I'm really sorry for breaking down. But, then, I know you, and I'm sure you don't mind."

Still not saying anything, the older man sat down next to his young friend on the couch. Placing a hand on his shoulder, he waited.

Taking his watch from his left wrist, the young man began cleaning it with his handkerchief. He wiped the moisture from the crystal and held it up to the light. Then he said in a sardonic tone, "You know, it's funny. Five people in her family have died of cancer. Five. Her mother, an aunt, and even her older sister—and she was only thirty-eight. I mean, when you face the real possibility that your wife could actually die—and she's only thirty-two years old—it sort of makes things like this seem pretty unimportant. Forty-six hundred dollars I paid for this watch—and I could have spent more—but I *had* to have a Rolex. Just like I had to have the Beamer. And the Armani suits. And the Bayliner ski boat. CDs and the stock portfolio and the mutual funds. We weren't just planning for the future—we had it all now. But if I lose her, I'm not sure I even care about living anymore."

173

Again the young man's voice broke. Still the older man said nothing. The silence grew, threatening to drown out the sounds that filtered in from outside—cars passing on the street, children calling to each other in play, and, from another portion of the house, the sound of a clock striking the hour.

"Does God get upset with us if we ask why?"

Finally the young man spoke again. "I really didn't want to come over here today. My wife—she almost forced me to. But thanks for just being there. Thanks for not preaching me a sermon. I don't know—somehow I just felt like you'd probably suggest I pray about it or tell me that somehow, from God's point of view, this was good. I just don't think I could have handled that. Thanks for being here for me. It helps."

Another pause, not as long this time. "But I still keep asking myself, why. Do you think God's punishing me—or punishing her because of getting involved with the curator?"

Finally the older man spoke, his voice quiet but firm. "I think we can lay that one to rest pretty quickly. Was your wife's developing cancer some kind of punishment for her getting involved with another man? Seems logical to me that if several members of her immediate family have had cancer, this thing probably developed long before that ever happened."

A look of relief crossed the young man's face. "Yeah—I guess that does make sense, doesn't it? I hadn't thought about it that way. I mean, it's just hard to think about things. Does God get upset with us if we ask why?"

The older man smiled. "Absolutely not. In fact, my kids used to ask me why a lot of the time. Now my grandkids ask me why—ask their parents why, too. We parents seem to be able to handle it when our kids ask, and I think God is a far more loving parent than we ever thought about being. I'm sure He doesn't always tell us why—sometimes it's probably too complicated for us to really understand. But I don't think He ever minds our asking."

The young man cleared his throat, dabbed at his eyes again with his handkerchief. He adjusted his position on the couch, then turned sideways to look directly at the man who had become his mentor. "You know, I've only known you a few months, but I think you really care about me. And I think you really are in touch with God.

"When we first started getting together—I'll have to be honest with you—I sort of looked down on you. I mean, you didn't drive an expensive car or wear designer clothes. You didn't have a lot of the things I've already been able to acquire. I was a vice president already—the youngest in my company's history—and I didn't even know what your title was. Here I've been climbing this ladder thinking I was headed for the top. I think you've shown me I've been climbing the wrong ladder. I mean, I've given my wife fashionable jewelry, a beautiful home, an expensive car. And if she dies, she can't take any of it with her. As far as that goes, I could drop dead of a heart attack tomorrow myself. You know, one of my co-workers had a heart attack—just a week ago—and he's in his late thirties. He survived, but it could have gone either way."

Again the young man was quiet for a moment as he looked toward the window in the room. "I mean, it's so hard—just thinking about this. The thought of losing her just makes me want to give up. It's amazing to me that that's not how she feels. I can't believe how courageously she took the news. It's upsetting. But for some reason it seems to have hit me harder than her."

"I don't have any pat answers," the older man said. "I think I may have told you about the time I almost lost my wife—she nearly bled to death when our first baby was born. It all happened so quickly. I didn't have time to think about my feelings. But afterward I just shuddered every time I thought about the prospect of life without her. I was about your age at the time—in fact maybe a few years younger. It really helped me think about what was important.

"At the time I'd had several people encourage me to get into some things where I could make a lot of money. I think coming close to losing someone who matters to me as much as she does gave me a different point of view as far as what really matters. I heard someone say once, 'You never see a hearse pulling a U-Haul trailer.' I guess that's just another way of saying 'You can't take it with you.' You can have all the money in the world, all the power in the world. But when you die, it's gone.

"Solomon talked about that once. He said that you can work and work and work to amass a huge fortune. Then you die and leave it to someone who comes after you. And who knows whether he'll be a wise person or a fool? How he'll use it? What he'll do with it?

"Now I don't think this means we shouldn't work hard or do the best we can. I think it comes down to what really matters in our life."

"It's hard to explain how I feel right now," the young man said. "I mean, part of me just wants to give up completely. Part of me wants to go on like before—sort of going for the gold. Then I guess there's another part of me saying that maybe everything that glitters isn't gold."

The room was silent again. Then the young man asked a question. "Did you ever feel like giving up? Somehow I can't picture you feeling that way."

The older man didn't answer for a moment. Instead he walked over to the roll-top desk in the corner of the room. Opening a drawer he took out a by-now-familiar stack of 3x5 cards. Returning to the couch, he handed them to his young companion.

"For a long time, I felt I'd *never* come to the place of giving up. Oh, at times I would become discouraged. But I was determined never to quit at anything. In fact, there were a lot of people who told me my encouragement kept them from quitting.

"I thought I understood what it meant to overcome feelings of despair. Then one day something happened. It all started with a phone call in the middle of the night. Within a matter of days it seemed like my entire life had come unraveled. I mean, I felt like Job. No, nobody died, but just about everything else that could come apart did. I felt like giving up. It involved my job, my family, some of my closest friends—plus, I developed pneumonia. Spent six weeks flat on my back. During that time I put these cards together, because for the first time, I really felt like giving up." The older man paused for a moment, and the young man looked at the cards. He realized that these were cards he had never seen during any of their previous meetings. He read them one at a time.

Luke 18:1 . . . Men ought always to pray and not give up.

Galatians 6:9 . . . Let us not be weary in well-doing, for in due time we shall reap, if we do not give up.

2 Corinthians 4:1 . . . Since we have received this ministry, as we received mercy, we must not give up.

2 Corinthians 4:16 . . . For this cause we do not give up. Though our outward man is dying, our inward man is being renewed day by day.

Hebrews 12:5 . . . My son, do not despise the discipline of the Lord, nor give up when you are rebuked by him.

The young man shook his head as he continued looking at card after card. Holding them out in front of him, he said, "You must have looked up every verse in the Bible about not giving up."

The older man smiled. "Just about. Something else helped me too."

Reaching to the bookshelf beside the couch, he pulled out a volume. The cover showed it to be a history of World War II. Opening the volume, he turned immediately to a place previously marked. The young man could see that one portion of the page had been circled with a blue highlighter.

Before handing him the book the older man said, "I'm sure you're familiar with Winston Churchill. I've always been sort of a history buff, and the thing that impressed me most about Churchill was his determination. I'd heard a story many times about Churchill speaking at a commencement, delivering the shortest graduation address ever—basically just saying, 'Never give up.' So, I decided to check it out.

"It turns out the war was just underway and things were looking pretty bleak for England. Churchill was speaking at Harrow School, one of those exclusive, typically English schools. Here's what he said."

He handed over the volume, and the young man's eyes immediately focused on the passage marked by the highlighter. "Never give in. Never give in. Never, never, never, never—in nothing great or small, large or petty, never give in, except to convictions of honor and good sense."

"There's a lot about Churchill's life I don't admire," the older man continued, "but you can't fault him on determination. He refused to give in. And when I felt like giving up, that helped me put feet to Jesus' parable about always praying and never giving up. Helped me understand how Paul could tell us to never give up—even when he was facing the most horrible of circumstances. And it helped me figure out the real implications of the promise about reaping in due season if we don't give up.

"Now when I was a kid, there were a lot of people where I grew up who farmed. I didn't have a lot of patience back then. It was hard for me to accept how long it took for seeds to grow when you planted a garden. Back then we didn't have microwaves, fax machines, or a lot of the instant things that are so much a part of our society today. Everything seemed to take a lot longer—especially growing things. It was hard for me to understand that you planted seeds today—and the harvest might be a long time down the road."

A look of understanding crossed the young man's face. "You know, that's exactly what my broker told me last week.

I've been after some quick earnings investments—the kind of thing you get into quickly and out of just as quickly—a lot of people have made quite a bit of money in options and commodities futures—things like that. But my broker told me that the smart investor is the one who takes the long-term perspective. He doesn't bail out when the market drops seventy points the way it did last Monday. Nor does he come to the conclusion that he'll be an overnight millionaire after the Dow Industrials gain fifty points two days in a row. He's in it for a long-term combination of income and growth.

"I guess one of the lessons I've learned from him is kind of similar to what I need to learn here. I was ready to get out of the stock market altogether when that big drop happened. I thought it was one of those deals like 1989. He kept telling me over and over. 'Don't panic. Don't panic. Don't give up.' I took his advice in the market, and I think you're telling me the same thing about life."

"I think there are two basic questions we have to ask ourselves: Who's really in charge, and does He care about me?"

The older man shifted positions on the couch. "Not only that. I'm not telling you as somebody who doesn't understand what it's like to feel like giving up. I've been there. Maybe not in exactly the same kind of way, but all the things that mattered most to me were shaken.

"I guess the closest thing I can compare it to is an earthquake. Several years ago my wife and I were in southern California. In fact, we were on the eleventh floor of a hotel just across the parking lot from Disneyland. We'd been on one of those tours the day before—the usual vacation attraction—where they simulate an earthquake.

"About two o'clock in the morning, my wife woke me up, and she was pretty upset. Said we were in an earthquake. First thing I did was tell her to go back to sleep. Then she said, 'Look at the television set.' The television set was actually dancing across the dresser where it had been sitting. I could feel the building swaying. The windows didn't shatter, but they were creaking and groaning. I went over and looked out the window. There was a swimming pool on the roof about eight or ten stories below us. The lights over the pool were swaying, and, I kid you not, there were waves three or four feet high in that pool! It was all over in about thirty seconds, but I'll never forget it. I mean, it shook everything."

"So it actually was an earthquake?"

"Pretty good sized one—did quite a bit of damage out in the Palm Springs area. Killed at least one person, I believe. But you know what surprised me? The attitude of California residents. The next day I talked to people in the hotel and other places where we went. I figured they'd all be blasé about it—I mean after all, they live in what most of us consider the earthquake center of the universe. But they really took it seriously. They didn't joke around about it."

"Did you feel differently after the earthquake? About earthquakes, I mean. Even about things in general."

"I think so. I think it reminded me who's really in charge. It's so easy for me to think I'm in charge—especially when I'm charging through life as fast as I can. Then something happens that reminds me of how little control I have over things. But I think that's why Jesus taught that we ought always to pray and never give up.' I think there are two basic questions we have to ask ourselves: Who's really in charge, and does He care about me?"

"That's a good way of putting it," the young man said. "I may not have put it in exactly those words, but that's sort of what I've been thinking—you know—ever since we got the word about my wife. I mean, isn't God big enough to stop this? Why did He let this happen to her?"

The young man idly flipped through the cards in his hand. He stopped, looked at another of the cards, pulled it out, and examined it more closely. Then he read the card aloud.

"'Hebrews 12:3 . . . If you want to keep from becoming fainthearted and weary, think about his patience as sinful men did such terrible things to him.' Does this have anything to do with what we were talking about?"

"It might," the older man replied, taking the card offered him. "I think this writer was talking about life as though it were a race we were running. Earlier in Hebrews 12 he refers to Jesus as the author and finisher of our faith. In other words, Jesus ran the race before us. He suffered far more than we ever will. He's an example and an inspiration to us not to quit. I think there's also an element of discipline in this verse and the ones that follow it. You played high school football, didn't you?"

"Yeah. I never was that great at it, but I sure enjoyed the competition."

"What did you like least about football?"

"The summer practices—two a day in August. It was a hundred degrees in the shade—hotter in the sunshine. We did all sorts of conditioning drills—and running, running, running all the time."

"That's what I remember about it, too. But you know what? Late in the fourth quarter of a close game, the discipline of those hot summer days sure paid off. The team that worked the hardest in those early drills was usually the team that didn't quit. Most often, they were the team that won."

"So you think maybe God's working us out a little bit for His team?"

The older man leaned back on the couch and smiled. "I'm not sure that's really for me to say. I think if I were in your shoes, I'd probably do two things. First, I'd make up my mind not to give up. I'd follow Jesus' advice, and Paul's too—even Churchill's. Second, I'd pray. I'd ask God what's going on, what I need to learn. I'd tell him how I feel. I'd be really honest with Him about how upset I was over my wife's cancer. I'd ask Him to show me what He wanted me to learn—especially about what really matters."

"But that's so hard to do," the young man said. "I'm not sure I can. In fact, I'm not sure I even want to."

At this point the conversation was interrupted by a knock at the door. "When are you two going to take us out to eat?" a voice asked.

"How about right now?"

13

NEVER FORGET

I can't believe what a great time we had at dinner—after I felt so horrible, the young man thought as he guided his BMW deftly through the early afternoon traffic. *I haven't laughed that hard in years—and I never realized some of the things my wife thought were funny. That One Minute Christian—he's a sly one. I had no idea he was such a dry wit. And his wife—what a dynamic lady! I mean, she's been through all kinds of grief. And never a word of complaint. After all that stuff they've been through—almost losing two children!—and what he's been through in his work, why I think I'd have given up a long time ago. I'm really going to miss these meetings.*

Steering his car off the freeway, the young man quickly drove the few blocks to the office of the man he referred to as the One Minute Christian. He thought about that title as he pulled into the parking lot next to his mentor's office. *The One Minute Christian. I think I've labeled him right. He wouldn't agree with me. But I think he is. Not the way I thought he was at first—he lives it one minute at a time.*

He warmly greeted the older man's secretary, who had opened the door just as he was about to enter. "Debra, your timing is incredible. What's your secret?"

"Observation," the secretary cheerfully replied, handing him a mug of steaming coffee. "I happened to look out the window just as you drove up. By the way, I'm sorry to hear about your wife. I hope and pray things work out OK."

"I feel better about them. I'm still worried—but I can't believe how much he helped me over the weekend." Nodding toward the door of the older man's office he asked, "Should I go on in?"

"Sure. He's expecting you."

The young man gently rapped on the door, then opened it and entered.

"You seem to be feeling better," the older man observed after the two men shook hands and were seated at the conference table.

"I can't thank you enough for this past weekend. You were there for me. You listened. And your wife was just an angel. She really encouraged Suzi. I don't think either one of us realized how low we were—until after we headed home. We agreed that we both had the most remarkable turnaround in feelings we've ever experienced."

"When's her next visit to the doctor?"

"That's what I need to talk to you about. We've been doing a lot of praying about this cancer thing—and we're doing everything we can medically too. Just like you suggested. I called a friend of mine in Houston—his wife works at M. D. Anderson Hospital. You know, they're one of the top cancer treatment centers in the country. We leave tomorrow to drive down. We're not sure what's ahead—maybe surgery, radiation, chemotherapy. Or how long it will take. But we're going after it now."

"Sounds like a smart move. A friend of mine once said, 'When you're in a boat in the middle of a lake and a storm comes up, you need to pray hard—and row hard for shore.'" Both men chuckled.

"Well, that's what we're doing."

"What about your job?"

"Interesting you should bring that up. I was reviewed yesterday—and it may be the very first blip in my upwardly mobile career. Seems I haven't quite been up to the boss's expectations. Then on top of that, I had to tell him about the situation with my wife. Explained that I needed to take at least a couple weeks of vacation, plus some personal days.

"Funny thing though—normally I'd be upset about missing work, no matter what. But I'm not sure that matters much to me any more. I've read a lot of books about success. But I don't think any of them prepared me for this.

"This past weekend really started me thinking about—you know—that business about what really matters, what's lasting. I told you before, I was always out for the gusto. The work, the fun, everything.

"Now I may have hit a curve in my upwardly mobile career path—and maybe that's not such a big bad thing after all. I don't see you working eighty hours a week trying to get ahead—in fact, how many hours do you work?"

"A lot less than I used to. I used to be a lot like you—driven, intense. I felt like I had to perform. But I think mainly I was trying to perform to win God's approval. I thought God expected me to do everything for everybody. Then I began to realize, over a period of time, that God loves me for who I am, not for what I do. I came to the place where I really started enjoying God. Before, a lot of what I did was motivated by guilt.

"One of the best ways to begin enjoying God is to start keeping track of all the things He does in our lives, then be sure to thank Him for them."

"I guess in a way I viewed God as sort of like my football coach in high school. He was great, and he was in charge, and he even cared about me in a way. But mostly he cared about winning and about how well I produced. If I didn't produce, he could always bench me and go with somebody else. I mean, I broke into the starting lineup because three other guys who were ahead of me at my position didn't produce. Well, two didn't produce, and one broke an ankle."

"Enjoy God? Now that's a novel concept," the young man interjected. "I never really thought about it that way. I guess I've always thought of God as someone to be endured. How did you get to the place where you could enjoy God? How can you do that?"

The young man's mentor leaned back in his chair, propped up his feet on the conference table, and clasped his hands behind his head. "Pardon me for being so casual. To tell you the truth, I think you've been the best illustration of one of the best ways to enjoy God—and as far as that goes, to enjoy life."

"Now that doesn't make sense," the young man said, a puzzled look on his face. "How could I possibly be an illustration of enjoying God? I just told you, I don't think I've ever even thought about the concept. How can you do something you've never thought of?"

"I didn't say you had thought of it or actually learned to enjoy God. I just said you illustrated it. What did you say when you first came in here today?"

The young man scratched his chin. "I don't know. 'Hello. Thanks for this past weekend.'"

"Ah-ha! 'Thanks'—you said thank you."

"That I did, and that's how I feel. But what's that got to do with enjoying God?"

"Quite a bit. In fact, I'm convinced that one of the best ways to begin enjoying God is to start keeping track of all the things He does in our lives, then be sure to thank Him for them."

"You mean like the little things we talked about when we had lunch at Plaza Tower?"

"That and the big things that He does for us as well. You see, for a long time I was known to the people around me as a positive person. But at times, my thinking was pretty negative. What happened was that I tended to focus on the bad things that were happening in life—the little disasters, the things that didn't go my way at work, or the hassles at home. There were a lot of things I needed to learn—like not getting caught up in envying other people when it seemed they had more than I did, forgiving people who hurt me instead of holding grudges against them—things like that."

"You mean, you had to work at not being bitter?"

"Don't we all?" The older man smiled. "But I had these two friends—very special friends. One was quite a bit older than I was, the other several years younger. Like me, they loved pizza. And they were close friends with each other. Although they were several decades apart in age, they both started doing something at about the same time—and that challenged me to try it."

The young man's face indicated intense interest.

"They started keeping a journal. Now they didn't write down a lot of rambling thoughts, but they faithfully recorded at least one good thing—big or little—God had done for them each day.

"Now here's the funny part. Even though I hadn't started doing this at the time, they both gave me some of the credit for encouraging them to get started. All I had done was share with them one of these verses I keep on these cards."

Taking a card from his shirt pocket, the gray-haired man handed it to his young friend. The young man took it and read from the card as if on cue: "Psalm 103:2 . . . Bless the Lord, O my soul, and forget not all His benefits" (NKJV).

The older man continued. "You see, I don't think it's enough just to say 'thank you' to God. I think we really start enjoying Him when we remember all the things He's done for us. And with my memory like it is, the only possible way to do that was to write it down—record these blessings in my Day Timer.

"Now, these friends of mine, whenever either of them felt discouraged or down in the dumps, would take out their journals and review them. They claim that's the best medicine for heading off discouragement, even depression. When times were really tough, the two of them would get together and compare notes."

"I'm still not sure just writing things down in a journal—or even entering them into a computer—will do that much to help me enjoy God," the young man countered.

"I'd probably agree with you. Even though I still think it's important to keep track of those blessings. I tend to look at this business of remembering benefits as one of life's important *nevers.*"

"Nevers? Now you're talking in riddles."

"Things like *never* give up, *never* forget."

"Oh, I get it. Sort of a way of reminding yourself?"

"Exactly. But I think the real issue, as I was about to say, is not just to store all our blessings on a notebook or in the hard drive of a computer. The real issue is to let those positive memories produce what I call an attitude of gratitude."

"Hey, I like that phrase. Attitude of gratitude. It's catchy. Did you coin it yourself?"

"No, I didn't. Actually I heard it from one of my profs back in graduate school—years ago. He was one of the most dynamic speakers I've ever heard—but I'll never forget hearing him share how at times he felt overwhelmed with depression, even to the point of giving up. What he told us was that, whenever he felt like giving up, he would immediately begin reviewing the blessings of God in his life. He called it the therapy of thanksgiving. He found it worked better than any medication. And he was a man who definitely enjoyed God. I don't know of anybody who has spent any significant amount of time with this man who didn't think he really enjoyed God."

The young man happened to glance at his Rolex. Shaking his head, he said, "I can't believe it. It's time for me to get going, and I feel like there's so much more to learn. But you know, I really think there's a difference in my life. Maybe there's a chance I can learn to enjoy God—sort of like I see you enjoying Him.

"It's really strange, isn't it? I came in here looking for the One Minute Christian. I figured you'd give me some kind of shortcut to spirituality—thirty-second prayers or one-minute worship, something like that. Instead, you taught me some pretty basic things: how to trust God, how to pray, why the Bible is important, and how it can make a difference in my life.

"But you didn't teach me a lot of religious stuff. What you did was show me that God loves me for who I am, not for performing or jumping through some religious hoops. And I think in the process you've opened my eyes to see what's really important. I've been wrapped up in things, in success. But you helped me see I can't take any of it with me. What were those two major things about love that we talked about?"

The older man was delighted that his student had remembered. "Whole-hearted love for God, and unconditional love for people."

"Let me write that down. I want to make it a priority to start remembering. Can I borrow a 3x5 card?"

The older man handed him a blank card, and he copied the two phrases.

"There's one thing I've been meaning to ask you," the young man said after he gave his friend a warm hug and a firm handshake. "That card on your bulletin board. What do those initials stand for?"

The older man looked at the card. It contained six initials.

P   A   M   I   T   P

"It's a motto. I learned it years ago. Remember those two women we discussed—Mary and Martha?"

"Yeah. Martha was the one who was all tied up in knots, worried about getting the dishes done."

"She and her sister are the ones who taught me about this motto: People Are More Important Than Projects."

"I get it now!" exclaimed the young man. "Martha was wrapped up in projects. She wanted to get the dinner cooked, dishes done, the house clean; but Mary didn't."

"No. She chose to sit with Jesus. I guess you could even say she was enjoying Him."

THE ONE MINUTE CHRISTIAN

"I guess that's better than any one-minute formula. It's still hard for me to figure, though, why you'd care enough to take time out of your schedule for me. I'm sure I've been a pain at times. But I guess you really believe in that motto. People *are* more important than projects."

"That's how some people have related to me," the One Minute Christian replied. "Most of all, that's the way the Lord is. Over the course of history, He has certainly pulled off some big projects—creating the world, rolling back the Red Sea, zapping some of those nations in the Old Testament. But the greatest project of all wasn't really a project; it was Christ loving us people so much that He died for us."

The young man's eyes grew moist. "Thanks for caring. I sure haven't arrived, but I know God cares. I know you do. I really hate that we won't be able to get together for a while."

"Call me from Houston," the older man replied as his young friend walked out the door. "Let's keep in touch." When he closed his door to return to his desk, he noticed that his eyes were moist, too.

* * * *

Outside the office building, night was rapidly falling. The young man started his BMW and drove out of the parking lot. A thousand thoughts seemed to be running through his mind at once. *Enjoy God. . . . People are more important than projects. . . . Who I am is more important than what I do. . . . You can't take it with you. . . . Never forget. . . . Never give up. . . . One day at a time. . . . Be yourself. . . . Have fun.*

He drove under the freeway and accelerated up the ramp. *Maybe I'm not as upwardly mobile as I thought. But maybe it doesn't matter that much. Who knows? If I keep working on what really matters, in a few years maybe I'll be a One Minute Christian.*

EPILOGUE

It's been a year since I last met with the young man who was the focus of this book. But in a sense, this is really *my* book, even though I've written it from the view of my young friend. You see, I went through a lot of the same struggles he went through. Oh, when I was growing up there was no such thing as baby boomers or even yuppies. Air travel and long distance calls were relatively rare. There were no fax machines, microchips, or space shuttles.

But there were still plenty of people given to the pursuit of things, following the motto "You can have it all if you just work hard enough." Entitlement, entertainment, expectations, and enlightenment were the driving forces behind many lives.

I could very easily have moved in the same direction. Plenty of people—family, friends, teachers, school guidance counselors—challenged me to "go for it."

"After all," they said, "you have an ability that can take you a long way."

I was somewhat younger than the young man in our story when I was challenged to alter my thinking. I don't remember a lot about the particular circumstances, but one statement had a dramatic impact on me. I think it originated with Jim Elliott, a young missionary, who gave his life in South America in 1956. He was the man who originally came up with the phrase Gil Phillips had heard from his dad: "Wherever you are, be all there. Live to the hilt every situation what you believe to be the will of God."[1]

But he said something else that impacted my life even more: "He is no fool who gives up what he cannot keep to gain what he cannot lose."[2]

Years before I had received the gift you cannot lose— genuine life. I had trusted Jesus Christ to forgive my sins.

And what about the young man who is the basis of our story? His plight is a common one—in fact, it is the *human dilemma.*

In their best-seller, *In Search of Excellence,* Tom Peters and Robert Watterman point to company after successful company in which success has come about through a focus on people. They list six crucial characteristics of people. The first of these, and the last, describe what I see to be the human dilemma as represented in the young man whose story I have told.

First, all of us are self-centered.[3] It is this self-centered-ness that is at the heart of a concept we'd like to pretend doesn't exist in our enlightened pop-psychology era. That concept is *sin.* Respected psychiatrist Karl Menninger put it this way: "In all of the laments and reproaches made by our seers and prophets, one misses any mention of 'sin,' a word which used to be a veritable watchword of prophets. It was a word once in everyone's mind, but now rarely have ever heard. Does that mean that no sin is involved in all our troubles?—sin with an "I" in the middle?"[4]

A second characteristic identified by Peters and Watterman was also shared by the young man. "We desperately need meaning in our lives, and will sacrifice a great deal to institutions that will provide meaning for us."[5]

1. Elisabeth Elliott, *Passion and Purity* (Old Tappan, N.J.: Revell, 1984), p. 80.
2. Elisabeth Elliott, *Shadow of the Almighty: The Life and Testament of Jim Elliott* (New York: Harper & Row, 1958), p. 15.
3. Thomas J. Peters and Robert H. Waterman, Jr., *In Search of Excellence* (New York: Harper & Row/Warner, 1982), p. 55.
4. Karl Menninger, *Whatever Became of Sin?* (New York: Hawthorne, 1973), p. 13.
5. Peters and Waterman, *In Search of Excellence,* p. 56.

So what did *I* have to offer this young man, who was searching so desperately for meaning, for answers for his life? The simple offer—one he welcomed, embraced, and applied—was not a philosophy, a religion, or a technique. It was a relationship with a person—Jesus Christ. A relationship based on trust. Coming to that relationship, learning to enjoy it—that's what this book has been about.

Some time ago, while talking with the senior acquisitions editor of a major publishing house, I asked, "What kinds of books seem to be touching the heartbeat of the book-reading public today?"

The reply, without hesitation: "Two kinds of books seem to have the most impact. One is self-help. The other is spirituality."

The One Minute Christian could be categorized as a book on spirituality. But spirituality is a broad concept. My purpose in *The One Minute Christian* is to be more focused.

Over the past thirty or so years I have studied the Bible, examined theological arguments, and considered the application of distinctively Christian principles to various areas of life. The goal of *The One Minute Christian* is to summarize a great deal of what I have learned—with the ultimate purpose of showing how being a Christian can meet our most basic need and give meaning and purpose to life.

By "Christian," I don't mean one who adopts a certain denominational tag, such as Baptist, Presbyterian, or Catholic. Nor am I speaking of one who conforms to a set of rules. After all, according to *The Day America Told the Truth*, most people today have edited the Ten Commandments down to their personally acceptable condensed version of four or five—and most of them have redefined those imperatives as simply helpful suggestions.[6]

What I mean by Christian is one who has come to a personal relationship with Jesus Christ, based on trust—one who understands who Christ is, what He achieved through

6. James Patterson and Peter Kim, *The Day America Told the Truth* (New York: Prentice Hall, 1991), p. 6.

His sacrificial death on the cross, how He rose from the dead the third day (a truth verified by unquestionable eyewitness evidence), and why that makes such a difference to people of the twentieth and twenty-first centuries.

The One Minute Christian is, like other books bearing similar titles, a simple compilation of what many wise people have taught me, plus what I have learned through personal study. Although my indebtedness to Kenneth Blanchard and Spencer Johnson of *The One Minute Manager* for the idea of this parable goes without saying, I want to acknowledge their creativity. I also want to assert that, in the process of learning from others and sharing with others what I have learned, I have been taught and have grown.

James Naisbitt in his unsettling book *Megatrends* observes, "We are drowning in information, but starving for knowledge."[7] What knowledge can meet our most basic hunger? For the young man of this book, it was the personal knowledge of Jesus Christ—coming to trust Him as Savior and friend; experiencing freedom from guilt and self-deception; learning to grow in Him; finding desperately needed meaning and purpose in relating Him to every area of life.

Today my wife and I have a comfortable life. We're involved in a variety of enjoyable activities—serving God and people. Almost every day I talk to individuals from all walks of life. Many of them are lonely, hurting. Some are at the point of despair.

I'm always glad to be able to point them not to a "One Minute Christianity" formula or a set of rules but to the Person who's made a difference in my life—who's kept me from giving up when things looked worse than bleak; who's given me enough adversity to keep me from being overwhelmed with arrogance; who's given me friends to tell me the truth, to care about me, to encourage me; who's taught me to recognize that, although I don't have all the answers, I know where to find them (at least the ones that matter);

7. James Naisbitt, *Megatrends* (New York: Harper & Row/Warner, 1988), p. 24.

who's reminded me frequently of the value of a cheerful heart and let me know in many ways that He loves me for who I am, not for what I do; and who's taught me that it's OK to enjoy God and people.

By the way, I don't wear a Rolex watch or drive a BMW. But I do have a good friend who wears a Rolex and another who drives a BMW 735i. Both of them love God and people a great deal. I thought it was important to say that so that none of us would get the idea that such material possessions are, in themselves, inconsistent with loving God and people.

And the young man? His wife is regaining her health. She went through major surgery, followed by radiation and chemotherapy—it was quite an ordeal. They may never have children, but their marriage has been healed. She's committed to him, and he to her, and they're now enjoying God and each other.

And his career? Well, it seems that aggressive young man in the office leap-frogged right over him into the next promotion. So after a few months he decided to leave the rat race to the rats. He has a new job working for a small brokerage firm. There are several other Christians in the office. They regularly get together to encourage each other—usually over lunch. Sometimes I get together with them.

The young man hasn't arrived, but he's certainly on the way. He understands that people are more important than projects—and he tries to put that into practice. He's learned to be himself. And to have fun. And I think he's learning to live life one day at a time. Who knows? Maybe *he's* the One Minute Christian.